CW00665605

KNIFE THROWING LIKE THE PROS

PETER KRAMER

SCHIFFER PUBLISHING

4880 Lower Valley Road • Atglen, PA 19310

Originally published as *Messerwerfen wie die Profis* by Wieland Verlag GmbH © 2018
Translated from the German by Ingrid Elser and John Guess

Library of Congress Control Number: 2020930946

Edited by Ian Robertson
Photos: Peter Kramer, Holger Reiff, Frank Salonius, Richard Sunderland
Cover design: Justin Watkinson
Layout: Buch-Werkstatt GmbH, Bad Aibling
Type set in Rockwell Std/Minion Pro/Franklin Gothic

Disclaimer: All statements and information in this book are given according to the best of the author's knowledge and belief. Neither the publisher nor the author can assume any liability for possible accidents or damage which may occur during practice.

ISBN: 978-0-7643-6063-3
Printed in China

Published by Schiffer Publishing, Ltd.
4880 Lower Valley Road
Atglen, PA 19310
Phone: (610) 593-1777; Fax: (610) 593-2002
E-mail: Info@schifferbooks.com
Web: www.schifferbooks.com

For our complete selection of fine books on this and related subjects,
please visit our website at www.schifferbooks.com. You may also write for a free catalog.

Schiffer Publishing's titles are available at special discounts for bulk purchases for sales promotions or premiums. Special editions, including personalized covers, corporate imprints, and excerpts, can be created in large quantities for special needs. For more information, contact the publisher.

We are always looking for people to write books on new and related subjects.
If you have an idea for a book, please contact us at proposals@schifferbooks.com.

Contents

A Note about Informality
Since knife throwers are used to addressing each other informally, this book also uses informal colloquial language. Knife throwers are a community, and the reader is cordially invited to participate in it.

Out of the east on an Irish stallion came bounty hunter Dan.
His heart quickened and burdened by the need to get his man.
He found Pete peacefully fishing by the river, pulled his gun,
*   and got the drop.*
He said, "Pete, you think you've changed but you have not!"
He cocked his pistol pulled the trigger and shouted, "Let it start!"
Pete drew a knife from his boot, threw it, and pierced Dan
*   through his heart.*
Dan smiled as he lay in his own blood, dying in the sun, whispered in
*   Pete's ear, "We cannot undo these things we've done."*
You're Outlaw Pete, you're Outlaw Pete, can you hear me?"

—Bruce Springsteen, "Outlaw Pete"

Preface

A really grim, bloody showdown in a great Springsteen song, right? Luckily, this duel between my namesake "Pete" and bounty hunter Dan has little in common with the reality of sportive knife throwing. For some considerable amount of time I played with the thought of writing this book that you now hold in your hands. What kept me from doing so was the fact that there is already a good reference book on the German market, written in 2010 by my much-valued friend and thrower, Dieter Führer.

While writing the first lines, I realized that both volumes complement one another splendidly, because Dieter's and my sports biographies show some differences and have different focal points. When I talked with Dieter about my plans, he encouraged me to continue; after all, there is not only one book about the sport of swimming. The result all the more confirms my assumptions: I tried hard to elucidate further aspects of our sport and not to repeat other views—for example, how to make your own throwing knife and throwing double axes—because they are already in Dieter's book.

In the US, sportive knife throwing and ax throwing have a distinctly longer tradition than in Europe, and especially in Germany. Thus, there is also a larger number of specialized books available in the States, which so far have not been translated into German. The trappers of the early nineteenth century trained their skills of precise throwing with their utility knives and axes to pass time outdoors and to compete with each other. This archaic sporting contest—the so-called Mountainman contest—is still held according to the traditional rules.

In Europe, knife throwing is either known from Wild West and adventure movies or from circus and vaudeville shows. In my early youth I came to knife throwing as a little fan of Wild West and Tarzan movies, and of movies about Native Americans, because the guys in the movies were able to do it so well. It looked "cool" and spectacular, and I absolutely wanted to learn how to do that.

This led to appropriating my beloved mother's kitchen knives every now and then to throw them at the pear tree in our garden. At that time I didn't know any better, and nobody thought this kind of sporting activity to be really praiseworthy—neither my mom nor the pear tree, and surely not the kitchen knives, which had to suffer so much more by this than they had to endure during kitchen work.

Well, you can guess that for this reason, I didn't receive any encouraging words or even accolades for these sporting achievements by my parents. On the contrary, there was rather regular trouble— actually totally justified. But during my early experiences as a "junior knife thrower" I at least realized two things: first, that the whole thing was outstanding fun, and second, that I apparently had a certain talent for this, because most throws—thrown "freestyle" from a distance between about 2 and 5 meters (6.5–16.5 ft.)—went quite well. My first scout knife, which I was allowed to possess at age fourteen, also quickly received its first flying lessons.

Later, already grown out of childhood, I trained throwing every now and then, but rather irregularly. Opportunities for this occurred on lonely beaches or in isolated forest clearings. This probably would have continued forever, but in 2004, while surfing the internet, I realized by chance that I was not alone with this craze! What a revelation! There are other knife maniacs like me, and they even have thrower meetings and competitions!

It took another year of training and preparation before I participated in my first competition (Pan-European Thrower Meeting 2005 in "Pullman City," a Wild West town in the vicinity of Passau, Germany).

When I reached the location I met extremely likeable companions, without exception. Back then there was not a single woman among the participants, and even today sportive throwing is about 85 percent a "big boys' thing." But women have caught up in the recent past, and their number has grown so much that in 2008 a separate women's rating was added to the competitions. I got to know great people with all kinds of backgrounds, representing a large number of other interests, ambitions, and hobbies. Former elite soldiers, police people, Wild West fans, martial experts, teachers, blacksmiths, circus riders, archers, computer scientists, merchants, artists, engineers, and craftsmen—we are really a colorful bunch.

Since those days I have enjoyed being part of this scene, and within the last decade I was able to make friends and keep friendships around the globe because we have one thing in common: we have lots of fun throwing things made of steel, and we share an ultimate enthusiasm for knives—one of the oldest tools in human history.

Currently in Germany, the image of a turning disk with a scantily clad lady draped over it is a cliché we sport throwers still have to fight against during daily practice. There is still a lot of work to do, which I am tempted to call "development aid." But sportive knife and ax throwing, getting right to the point, is a fantastic and demanding precision sport—thus the Brits simply and fittingly call it "target sport."

Apart from lurid show elements, sports-oriented knife throwing can be compared to archery or sport shooting with projectile weapons.

We sport throwers stand in front of the target at an exactly measured distance and aim at hitting the black center of the target disk to receive five points for our maximum rating. At the end of the competition we have objectively measurable, clear results, and points that stand up to comparison with other contestants, as well as with other shooters in the local gun club of the neighboring town or village.

Actually, everything is quite simple, and this simplicity almost bestows an air of Zen on sportive knife throwing: there is only the "here and now," the thrower, the throwing weapon and the target, and nothing more. In contrast to some other sport disciplines where, after some time, you are glad when the stressful training unit is finally coming to an end, with sportive knife throwing you just don't want it to end at all.

Learning how to throw knives and axes is no magical thing. As in every kind of discipline, sport throwing is built up systematically, starting with light basic exercises and going on to more difficult and demanding throws from longer distances onto small targets. And this is also the distinct difference to the show throwers in the circus and vaudeville, who land stunningly precise hits from relatively short distances (i.e., from between 2 and 3 meters [6.5–10 ft.] away).

During our standard contests, we sport throwers move at distances of up to 7 meters (23 ft.), and in Russian contests even up to 9 meters (29.5 ft.) away from the target disk. For the viewer this makes sport throwing very interesting, spectacular, and attractive. With the throwing ax you move even farther away into the 10-meter (33 ft.) region.

The beautiful thing about it is there are hardly any restrictions on age or other limits. In the US there is a thrower who participates in contests from his wheelchair. And this is not apart from the common contests in some kind of Paralympic special assessment, but right in the middle of the action and in direct competition with other sports people without any handicap. When you have a certain basic talent for throwing movements, you will quickly learn the basics of the sport knife. For example, you are able to hit a tennis ball into a pail from about 3 meters away. Can you do this? Then go on; you have just managed the qualifying exam! Welcome to my world!

Peter Kramer

Acknowledgments

For Jerry (+ 12/06/2016), Dieter, Werner, Walter, Norbert, Gregor, Christian, Daniel, Frank, Markus, Roland, Michael, Kari and Frank Salonius, Adam, Jan, Duri, Little John, Richard, Dan "the man," Jiri, Stany, Pierre, Jonathan, Michel "Le Bison Fou," Philippe, Pascal, Benjamin, Jean-Pierre, Bruno, Geronimo, Americo, Gaetano, Oronzo . . . and all other dear friends who just don't come to my mind at the moment. You are all brilliant!

1 The Throwing Knife as Sports Equipment

Are these trick knives that always stick?
*(Question of an interested boy after watching
one of my throwing demonstrations)*

The Right Choice

For purely logical reasons, at this point I would like to start with a discussion of our sports weapons. Only when you know what materials we deal with in our sport can you better imagine how sportive throwing itself works. What the racing machine is for the cyclist, the precision bow is for the archer, or a good mask, flippers, and snorkel are for the sports diver, these essential things are our knives for us throwing-sports people. They are our sports kit and basic equipment.

I also want to mention just for your reassurance that financially, knife throwing is a rather low-priced kind of sport. The purchase of three throwing knives of good quality and suitability is in the range of about $110 and thus surely doesn't drive any interested person immediately to the brink of ruin. Additionally, I want to remark that this purchase is very probably done only once, because a good throwing knife doesn't become "all used up" over many years, not even with frequent, regular use as a piece of sports equipment—given some rationality during training and some material maintenance. What runs up some costs among us sport throwers is traveling around the globe to attend our yearly contests, international championships, and thrower meetings. Throwers with mechanical skills quite often make their own throwing knives, but I will leave this aspect aside.

Almost any kind of sport requires some basic kit with the necessary pieces of sports equipment; for us sport throwers, this means throwing knives. Thus the first premise when buying a good throwing knife ought to be "I am too poor to buy junk!"

Now, what are the qualities of a reasonable throwing knife? Against the background of pure sports activities, a throwing knife has the sole task—after a successful throw—of biting into the target disk with a distinctive sound, similar to that of a tennis serve ("thunk!" for soft wood or "chock!" with somewhat harder wood), and sticking there. Our throwing knife doesn't have to be suitable for anything else. Accordingly, this kind of knife really is more a piece of sports equipment than a weapon, since the blade edges of most knife models are completely blunt for practical reasons.

To illuminate one important and quite essential aspect of our "hardware" in more detail, I now invite you to a brief thought experiment: imagine in front of you on a table a Ping-Pong ball (super lightweight!) and a solid rubber ball (quite some mass, about 10 ounces). Your task is to choose spontaneously one of these balls, which you then use for an aimed throw as far and as hard as you can. Which ball would you choose? Is your choice reasonable? Think hard!

In the end, one fact is absolutely clear: the Ping-Pong ball may be very light, but this doesn't make throwing it easier at all. But with a bit of startup, you will probably throw the massive rubber ball farther than 30 yards.

Lineup: Substandard throwing knife with a 4¾-inch blade (*top*) and two excellent, functional throwing knives: the "Kari Salonius Custom Thrower" (15 inches, *center*) and the "Joe Darrah Brokenfeather Custom Thrower" (13 inches, *bottom*)

What does this result mean for the choice of the right throwing knife? The answer is quite simple: a good throwing knife needs mass—and thus also weight—material strength, and length. Conversely, you may leave aside the numerous "light metal junk" items proffered as "ideal throwing-knife starter set, super lightweight, stainless steel" and such offers with similar descriptions. As we just found out, a functional throwing knife should, if possible, neither be too light nor too small. What is left then?

We know that a (nonaerodynamic) body can be thrown in a controlled way over long distances only if it has a minimum weight, and thus mass. When applied to a throwing knife, this mass always results from a certain relation of length to material thickness.

A good throwing knife should not fall short of a length of 30 centimeters (11 inches) if possible, or at least not be short of that by much. Second, it ought to put a weight of at least 10½ ounces on the scale; better is a weight between 12 and 16 ounces. For our contests, only such throwing knives are allowed that are at least 9 inches long. By the way, so far there are no restrictions with respect to maximum length; hence in theory you could, according to the current rules, even throw a sword, as long as its blade is not wider than 2⅓ inches. But there are already thoughts about introducing such a limit.

Against this backdrop, a large part of the thin metal offered on the market is immediately excluded from consideration. Of course, our competition rules limit the large variety of throwing weapons offered on the market, but this is only of advantage for you, your successful training, and your wallet. In my opinion, it can clearly be seen from the overall selection in the specialized shops that throwing sport is still a quite young type of sport. The choice is immense, but only about 5 percent of the wares are really useful.

In addition, I have to mention a further and important aspect: there is no difference between a "beginner's knife" or a "starter knife" and the throwing knife of an experienced thrower after many years of competition. The difference is in the fact that most of the competition sport throwers (such as myself) at some point start making their own designs and creations or have them produced. These are then perfectly suited to the individual person and their individual way of throwing. Please, provide yourself with a reasonable piece of sports equipment right from the beginning, because good throwing knives are really not expensive.

In addition, I recommend a package purchase of three or four identical knives of your choice, because this gives you the chance to

2. The "Pro Balance Thrower" by Cold Steel: robust, full weight (about 16 ounces), and a good length (13½ inches). With these characteristics, in my opinion it is currently one of the best throwing knives. Because of its symmetrical spear shape and its blunt sides, it can be used without danger of injury and is extremely insensitive and rather cheap (less than $44).

3. The "Perfect Balance Thrower," also by Cold Steel; my former contest throwing knife. Overall length is about 13 inches. A modern replica of the legendary "Bowie Axe" by Harry McEvoy of the 1960s, with a satisfying weight. You ought to be a bit careful when handling it because the blade edge is sharpened. To minimize the risk of injury, you have to clamp it into a vise and use a file or angle grinder to make the edge blunt up to about 2 inches from the blade tip.

4. The Condor "Dismissal." It is more than 14 inches long, is cheap (about $33), and has a handy symmetrical spear shape. The knife is made of nonstainless, tough carbon steel.

5. The "Artistenwurfmesser" ("Artist's Throwing Knife") by Haller: 13⅓ inches long, sufficient weight, and very pleasant to throw. The knife tip is indeed absolutely pointed like a needle, but it doesn't stay that way for a long time during rough use. Nevertheless, a great throwing knife.

6. The "Ziel" by John Bailey. My American thrower friend John designed the symmetrical shape of this model. It has a length of 13⅓ inches and a weight of around 12¾ ounces—about everything a good throwing knife needs.

7. The "Faka" (Portuguese for "knife") by Dalmo Mariano of Brazil. My very first competition throwing knife; it has a very simple design and is made of a plain piece of sheet steel. It has a length of 14 inches and a weight of almost 14 ounces, but for my taste the blade is too thin. Apart from its not very convincing looks, the knife can be thrown well, and I owe this model my first successes in competitions.

8. The "Rough Rider Bowie." The shape and length of this throwing knife can almost be called optimal—but not the material. With a length of 14 inches, it is absolutely suited for competitions, and if the blade were made of reasonable steel this knife would be third or second on my hit list. On the other hand, it is extremely cheap and good initial equipment for getting a whiff of our sport. The "Rough Rider Bowie" can be obtained for as little as $17.

9. The "True Flight Thrower" model by Cold Steel. With a length of only 12 inches, it is a bit short for my taste, and the handle is a bit too thick. It can be thrown quite well by its blade, but you have to train for this because its blade is sharpened; thus it is of only limited suitability as a competition knife. By the way, all Cold Steel knives are made of tough, nonstainless carbon steel and are really robust and insensitive. Smaller nicks and dents can be filed off in a matter of seconds. Apropos, the best and toughest blade steels are not stainless.

These eight models are examples of throwing knives produced in series; of course, this results in a low price. Generally it can be said that one will be well provided with them, especially at the beginning of a thrower's career. If you have developed a sophisticated throwing technique in later years, you can also confidently throw a handmade knife.

My current throwing knives (*starting at left*): "The Shark" (Werner Lengmüller), "Custom Thrower" (Kari Salonius), "Outlaw Pete" custom competition knife (Peter Kramer), "Pro Balance" (Cold Steel), two small knives by Gil Hibben, "Mountain Man" / "The Tracker" (Kari Salonius), individual item by Kari Salonius (800 grams, 15¾ inches), "Perfect Balance" (Cold Steel), and "Arminius" (Kari Salonius)

Knife Models of Small Manufacturers

Werner Lengmüller Knives

Here I recommend in first place the handmade products of my thrower friend Werner Lengmüller from Wenzenbach, close to Regensburg, Germany. Currently, Werner is one of the world's best knife and tomahawk throwers and, among other accolades, holds the US record in the "walk back" discipline with the tomahawk. He indeed knows very well what he is doing. His handmade knife models are highly functional, extremely shapely, and absolutely indestructible. The high-tensile tool steel he uses is usually at least 5 millimeters (0.2 inches) thick and is equivalent to the material used to make normal tool hammers. Has anybody among you ever seen a broken hammer head? That's it.

On the other hand, Werner's knives are created by pure manual work. Piece by piece they are created in his workshop with a lot of love for detail. In my opinion, currently they are the best a sport thrower can get. It is logical that you can't get such knife models at a discount price. On the other hand, we live in a world where some people stand in line in front of electronics stores to be able to spend a whopping $800 for the latest model of a certain mobile phone. A good throwing knife made by Werner costs about $133, but it is worth the price—without any discussion.

Please don't be angry or disappointed if it takes a few days or sometimes even weeks before Werner responds to your inquiry. He has to lead a crafts enterprise as his main job, and now he receives a lot of orders from all over the world and maintains waiting lists.

A special characteristic of Werner's knives is the obvious spinning rings on many of his models. No, these are not telescopic sights! But you can use them to rotate your knives around your index finger like

A small number of models by Kari Salonius (*left to right*): Viking bearded ax with wolf head, Norse tomahawk with horse head, Rambo machete (can also be thrown well), classic throwing knife, and a "Mountainman-Tracker Thrower"

a cowboy. This looks very cool and also loosens your inner tension during competition—similar to a tennis player who bounces the ball a couple of times prior to a serve or a soccer player who, prior to a free kick or penalty kick, turns the ball around a couple of times and moves it around until its location and the way it looks are okay for him or her (and I always thought that the ball is equally round on all sides!). It is the same with us throwers: we just like to turn our knives around a finger.

Kari Salonius "The Axeman" Knives and Tomahawks

Kari Salonius of Finland (www.axeman.us) lives in Vantaa, close to Helsinki, and has become a dear friend to me over many years. In addition, he has a wonderfully dry and original humor. He is also a very versatile person: a black-belt holder in jiujitsu, a retired blacksmith, and a Wild West fan. As a trained smith he knows masterfully how to treat hot iron and makes the most-beautiful knives and axes in manual work.

The knives from Werner Lengmüller's workshop are nicely shaped, have excellent flying qualities, and are almost indestructible.

But sometimes this results in quite bizarre models. A short time ago he couldn't resist and made a "Mickey Mouse Tomahawk": a fully functioning Native American war ax with a faithful reproduction of Mickey Mouse as an ax head!

As a Wild West man, Kari especially makes high-quality utility knives and throwing knives in one—thus, classical mountain man knives. The blades always have a thickness between 5 and 8 millimeters (0.2–0.3 inches) and are thus quite indestructible as long as you don't put them on a rail track—even in this case I'm not sure whether they wouldn't derail a train. But please don't try this out yourself! By the way, most of Kari's knives have handles of untanned deer skin.

In case you want to purchase one of his knives, this works like in an internet mom-and-pop store: you tell Kari via mail which of the models you'd like to have (for example, "on the first page, the second from above to the left; I'd like to have three of them!"), then you'll receive a price for them and a bank connection. Please pay this price in advance (you have to trust Kari this far; he is an absolutely honorable person), and about four days later the post will deliver an oblong package from Finland. Shipping works smoothly!

The "Le Sphinx" by Pierre Cazoulat of the Bretagne is a nicely shaped throwing knife with good flying characteristics.

By the way, Kari speaks English very well, which makes conversation during the process of ordering much easier.

Pierre Cazoulat: Le Sphinx

The Breton Pierre Cazoulat has also been a very good thrower friend for many years and is a world-class top thrower, as well as the 2011 World Champion of the IKTHOF (International Knife Throwers Hall of Fame) for knife throwing. He is a man who can be at his top performance especially at longer distances between 16 and 23 feet.

After many years as a nature and hunting guide in Canada, he took over his parents' shop in Callac-de-Bretagne in 1997 at age twenty-nine. Besides household wares, the shop also sold knives and hunting and fishing gear. Here he found his way back to knife throwing, which he had already extensively trained in as a little boy.

Today Cazoulat produces his own throwing-knife models, which he designs himself. The top model, "Le Sphinx," with its pleasing hunting-knife shape, has very pretty looks; it is 13¾ inches long and has a weight of 15 ounces. It is one of my favorites for getting started in this type of sport. The model can be purchased easily via internet dealers or Cazoulat's website (www.pierre-cazoulat.com).

28

Learning How to Throw Knives

The Important "Basics"

How do I start? At the very beginning! But all joking aside: every type of sport whose results in the end look complicated while at the same time fascinating and playful is built up systematically. Thus we always move from the easier to the somewhat more difficult element—and at the very end to the most-demanding grades of difficulty. For comparison: a newbie in high diving without any prior knowledge won't directly and totally free of fear go straight up to the 10-meter platform and, without hesitation, launch into a flawless three-and-a-half somersault, at the end of which he or she plunges exactly vertically into the water without splashing. In the figurative sense we start with jumping from the pool's starting block. Our beginner's exercise will give you a good feeling for how it is to let the knife slip out of your hand during launch.

You have a block of wood, a thick and soft panel, or a tree disk of soft wood? If so, then this target you now put directly in front of your feet. As an alternative, you stand on a lawn area—if possible, with soft ground and without rocks or pebbles, because these may damage your blade tips. After a short "interim" with respect to the gripping technique, we will continue immediately.

Sportive knife throwing in principle is a quite "lawless" kind of sport. This just means that there is no regulation in the world of knife throwers that basically tells you to grab or hold a knife only in a very specific way.

Holding: side pinch at left, hammer grip on the right

Take the knife at the handle into your throwing hand and just hold it the way that's most comfortable for you. Don't hold it too loosely, but don't hold it in a cramped way either. Take it in your hand as if holding a small hammer used for carefully hammering a nail into a wooden plank. Some throwers without hesitation and instinctively put their thumb on the handle's back (this is the so-called hammer grip).

If this is a comfortable gripping technique for you, then you are free to stay with it; there is no "right" or "wrong" here. If possible, take care not to let too much of the handle stick out at the rear end of your fist, because this may lead to "getting caught" on it while launching the knife. The elementary difference between both main gripping techniques—the side pinch and the hammer grip—besides where you put your thumb, is that there is an additional biomechanical component that is decisive for the launch attitude.

For the hammer grip, the thrower has to turn his or her wrist to the right almost 90 degrees (lefties correspondingly have to turn it to the left) for the thumb to be in line with the forearm. This position in

The short whiplash throw onto a lying target

The short whiplash throw toward an upright standing target

turn distinctively reduces the mobility of the wrist in such a way that it is almost arrested at the end of the throwing movement when the knife leaves the hand. Both factors—the resting thumb as a counterbearing to the rotational movement of the knife, as well as the almost rigid wrist of your hand—with the hammer grip lead to a distinct slowdown of the knife's rotation. This has its advantages, but also disadvantages, which I will explain in more detail later.

Just make a little practice test without holding a knife in your hands: if the heel of your hand points forward as if waving goodbye you feel how movable your wrist is. But if you turn the edge of your hand forward as with a karate chop, you will immediately realize a distinct restriction of mobility vertically.

In comparison, with the side pinch, the heel of your hand points in the direction of throwing, because with this technique, only in this way can the knife fly in the desired direction while rotating vertically neat and straight. Thus with the side pinch, the wrist is much more flexible during launch. This or that thrower may add another additional "snapping" impulse to the knife in this way during the flowing motion—in most cases totally instinctively and automatically.

In the images (*right*) you can clearly see what the hand position looks like during the side pinch: during launch, the knife slides out of your hand between the thumb and the joint of your index finger; while holding and taking aim, the pinky doesn't touch the knife handle any more. For clean vertical rotations of the knife, during launch the heel of your hand points forward, and correspondingly the back of your hand faces backward. Thus the wrist is "free" and, as a lever, can add additional angular momentum to the throw.

But here you need to be careful, because in case you overdo the wrist snapping, the knife rotates too fast. The clear advantage of the side pinch throw is mainly that this throwing technique can be adjusted exactly to the throwing distances of contests. If you are well trained, no valuable distance to the target is lost, and you stand quite exactly just behind the particular mark. With the side pinch we throw our contest distances as follows:

3 meters (approx. 10 ft.): one rotation of the knife

5 meters (approx. 16½ ft.): the knife rotates two times

7 meters (approx. 23 ft.): an additional, third rotation of the knife

For clean and vertical rotations of the knife, the palm of your hand faces forward when launching the knife. Correspondingly, the back of your hand is oriented backward.

With this, the side pinch is the most common gripping technique.

Although hammer grippers often point out the supposedly better possibilities for steering throws by means of the thumb position, I personally am unable to see or use this advantage when trying. But it surely is a pure matter of taste and also a matter of habit. During contests I often see that sport throwers with this technique run into trouble with respect to distances. Just the basic throw with one rotation already needs almost 4 meters (13 ft.); the throw with two rotations needs at least 6 meters (19.5 ft.). This doesn't make experimenting with the material and the necessary knife rotations easier, while as a "side pincher" I always stand exactly at the mark. But I have come to know talented competitors who are able to switch between both techniques even in the middle of a contest as they see fit. This really commands my great respect.

Also important: if you throw an asymmetrical throwing knife, always hold your knife in a way that the blunt back is facing forward, and never the sharpened edge. The reason for this is very simple: if you are throwing

Dieter Führer from Schongau, Germany, in his seventies, is still an absolute top thrower at a world-class level. He prefers the hammer grip technique with the thumb resting on the handle's back.

series and only toward a single target, in the "worst case"—the collision of two knives—the knife thrown last can hit only the handle of the knife already sticking in the target with its insensitive back. Usually not much happens in this case, and your knives will stay almost undamaged. But if you throw with the blade edge forward, it is immediately clear that in case of a collision, deep irreparable nicks, cracks, and dents are almost preprogrammed, because the edge is much thinner and much more sensitive than the thick, blunt blade back.

There is a second reason for throwing the knife with the back facing forward, even though this may not be quite comprehensible for you right at the beginning. The back side of asymmetrical knives quite often has a bowie eagle's nose, which in case of not enough rotation "bites" into the wood almost like a hook. This happens even when the throw was perhaps not powerful enough or didn't have enough angular momentum.

Now take up your throwing position: a casual and relaxed lunge. Between the tip of your throwing knife with outstretched arm and the target on the ground in front of you is a distance of about 15 to 20 inches—not much more if possible. Hammer grippers add about another 16 inches to this.

The "Indiana Jones" Basic Exercise

Launching the knife—as a series of motions—can very well be compared to swinging a whip smoothly and dynamically. Imagine you are Indiana Jones and perform a throwing, swinging whip movement with your throwing arm in the direction of the target wood lying in front of you.

35

As can be seen in this rotation sequence, swinging backward and throwing is done in a continuous, fluid movement.

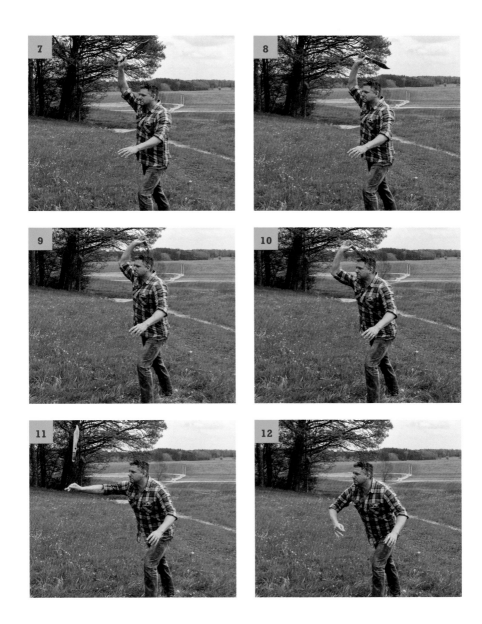

To make things easier, you should already have chosen a specific point on the target that you now aim at.

You briefly aim at the target, almost like a carpenter who, prior to hitting a nail, checks the direction of the hammer blow once more. Then you strike out calmly and just once; this means that under no circumstances do you weave backward and forward with your torso while making multiple striking movements.

The rest is purely a matter of feeling, which you simply have to try. At some time during the whipping motion, there is a brief point in time when you will let go of the knife. Don't consciously think about when this may occur. When throwing a tennis ball at a tin can, you wouldn't agonize when to best let go of the ball; you would just do it automatically.

The knife's handle glides from your hand, then after launch the knife automatically makes a quarter turn and finally sticks in the wood or the lawn directly in front of you. Warning! If it sticks in your foot afterward, you definitely made a mistake. (Don't be afraid; this won't happen. But this little joke simply had to be made.) With this exercise you will directly and quickly develop a good feeling for how to let the knife glide out of your hand. At the same time, this initial throwing exercise is totally free of any danger to you, because you don't have to be afraid of a bouncing knife in case the throw was a failure.

You may take some more time for your first basic exercise with the target lying directly in front of you. This way the movement will become second nature to you, and after a while will feel absolutely natural and "right."

Extracting

Important for now and the future: when pulling the thrown knife out of the target wood, never lever sideways! At best, only the tips of your thrown objects get bent by this, but in worst case they will break. Thus you should immediately and from the start get used to pulling your knives straight from the wood while using your other hand to counter with corresponding pressure.

This course of action is especially reasonable for a freestanding target, because in case you forget to press against it, the target can easily fall toward you while you are turning away from it! This doesn't look especially competent but rather somewhat slapstick, and it reminds one of the great comedians of the era of silent movies—apart from the danger of the wooden target falling onto your shank or heel.

In case of a blade sticking very firmly in the wood, it is actually tolerable to lever it vertically upward and downward, because this way it usually loosens by itself.

Never bend to the left or right and never twist the knife; when pulling the knife from the target, lever only in the direction of the blade edge, if at all. It's better to pull only vertically while at the same time pressing against the target.

After some time of initial practice, you ought to look for some smaller targets on your target wood or on the lawn that you would like to "harpoon," such as clover leaves, small colorations on the wood, or a playing card. This way you can start aimed throwing, which in the long term is the main criterion of sportive throwing.

To immediately continue methodically reasonable training, at this point we arrive at another elementary part of our sport: the throwing target.

3 The Target

There is an absolutely ironclad law that every sport thrower has to adhere to without any compromises: we never ever throw at living objects! This rule even includes trees, because these are living too! The pear tree in the garden of my childhood days forgave me, I hope, prior to its death. Trees are indeed injured on their bark by thrown knives, and this allows parasites and vermin to enter. And we sport throwers don't want to be the reason for forest decline.

So now there is the question of what an optimum target for throwing has to look like. Please refrain from buying an off-the-shelf "knife thrower target," which sometimes can be obtained from dealers. You would only be hopping mad. These boards are usually as thin as a

The target for knife throwing in an ideal case is made of soft material such as poplar wood.

Handmade target on a board
construction, providing the possibility
of exchanging tree disks repeatedly

dartboard and consist of pressed cardboard. Such a thin board survives no more than just a single throw of one of my contest knives and then breaks into two parts. I would rather not imagine what would happen if I threw a tomahawk at this type of target.

On the other hand, the elaborate construction of a turning disk for the scantily clad female assistant is also out of the question from the very beginning. Luckily, I have to say, because we can't have everything!

The actual work effort is by far less for us. Best suited for our sports-oriented throwing training is a sufficiently large and thick tree disk of softwood. To get this we only have to ask at the local timber yard whether some suitable trees are about to be felled anywhere.

Targets of Soft Wood from Deciduous Trees

Poplar wood or basswood is ideal. This is good for us, because almost no one really wants to have the former, since it is neither good as firewood nor as construction timber. Poplar is exceptionally soft and, in a fresh state, provides us with the most wonderful hitting sound you can imagine: a gentle "thunk" as with a soft serve during a tennis game. The best reward for a successful throw!

The simplest construction, which is also the quickest one to make, consists of a softwood disk about 20 inches in diameter and about 6 inches thick. On its backside or its sides you can attach simple wooden boards by means of chipboard screws, in such a way that they form a large "A." Please take care that the target disk's center (the "bull's eye," which you would like to hit) is at a height of about 51 to 63 inches when you are setting up the construction.

Now you screw on another wooden panel or two at the sides of the disk to support the target on its back after setting it up—finished! At the end this will look a bit like a painter's easel, and, like an easel, it may also be tilted backward a bit.

Important for your understanding: the force and the vehemence of the thrown knife for the most part are taken by the soft target disk and absorbed. This means that the supporting legs of the construction—

With hard concrete floor or similar ground cover, it makes sense to provide a soft base to prevent knife damage in case of misses.

Targets at the beach made from driftwood. Moist, soft wood and perfect generous surroundings for training result in an ideal ambience—when you are almost alone there.

the aforementioned wooden panels—don't have to be extremely thick, heavy, or bulky, because they have to carry only the disk's weight.

With respect to impact energy, they also don't have to endure much because there is hardly any. After all, we are not throwing bricks! A thickness of about 1 to 1½ inches is sufficient for the legs and results in a target that is lightweight and easy to transport. When the target stands upright, as a test simply hit against it with the flat of your hand at half your strength. If it still stands afterward, it will also survive your training throws without taking any damage.

With a simple wooden construction you can also put up several disks next to each other in such a way that two throwers can train at the target simultaneously. The approach to this is almost identical: the backsides of the wooden disks are simply screwed onto the wooden construction, and then the whole thing is erected so that your targets are at the desired heights. Slabs and screws don't cost a fortune at the hardware store, meaning that your construction will always remain a quite inexpensive source of joy.

Besides that, tree disks of softwood are usually pure waste products for the timber industry. Often you can even get them for free from a sawmill. In case there is no such business in your vicinity, here is a somewhat morbid tip: in case there is a crematory in your area, ask where the coffins for instant cremation are built. For reasons of cost, these are often made of poplar wood because it is light and soft and thus burns quickly. If you are lucky, you may find what you are looking for there.

Targets of Coniferous Wood

The second choice is coniferous woods, such as spruce, pine, larch, or fir, which are also soft but have one disadvantage you can feel with your hand: resin. Resinified blades are awfully sticky and will turn your throws into so-called "gluey" throws. With these, your hands stick a tiny bit too long to the blade or handle and cause a throw toward the ground. By the way, this can also happen with sweaty hands or moist leather handles (a little bit later in the book, I will show you what to do to counter this). As an alternative to not having anything at all, a coniferous tree disk is still a good and useful solution that I also use every now and then.

A log pile in the forest as a target for training has to be taken with a pinch of salt. In case of misses, the knives may simply vanish between the logs, never to be seen again.

All other kinds of trees with leaves are excluded from our purposes because these woods are too hard to be targets. Although I know some throwers who intentionally throw only at very hard wood, because they believe that their throws become more precise this way, I don't share this kind of training philosophy. In my opinion, our knives are unnecessarily stressed and worn down this way, especially when there is a failure in throwing. During sportive competitions we are usually allowed to throw at softwood disks. But sometimes the expression "softwood" also includes the aforementioned coniferous woods and even the somewhat harder stone pines that Americans often throw at.

Even at the beach you can practice throwing quite nicely. Wood often lies around there, and you can build a suitable target from it. But be careful: failures often directly hit the sand. Like moles, your knives like to slide underneath the surface of the sand, sometimes almost 3 feet deep! Keep the exact place in mind and don't lose eye contact, then immediately stop your series of throws, walk over to the spot, and start digging. Until now I have always been able to find my blades again, but sometimes it can take up to ten minutes. You had best aim well!

Especially when you're training in a forest, it has to be absolutely guaranteed that you will never get surprised by suddenly appearing passersby or bicyclists. It is absolutely clear: a hit between the shoulder blades ruins the day for any pedestrian (just kidding!). Practice only at a place providing sufficient long-distance view.

Second: A stack of logs is suitable only for really experienced throwers, because you have to hit very accurately. If a knife inadvertently flies or falls into a gap between the logs, it is usually irretrievably lost, because some of these stacks stay in the woods for many years. This is all the more true for the front end as a target!

Safety always comes first when placing a target. More about this in the next chapter.

4 Safety

In the course of many talks with news reporters and other media representatives, regularly and seemingly instinctively I have been asked the same question: "Isn't knife throwing awfully dangerous?" In these cases I like to answer with a counterquestion (even though this is seen as impolite): "Would you put this question to an archer training in a sports club?" This really makes some conversational partners quiet and leads them to think about the actual danger when throwing knives.

A wide, open area is ideal for training outdoors.

Of course especially lay people always link knives emotionally with bare, pure danger. And, of course, throwing knives are indeed serious weapons that may cause immense damage when misused. But when reduced to the smallest common denominator, thrown knives—in direct comparison to a shot arrow (which may easily fly more than 110 yards)—have a much-shorter range and thus, seen matter-of-factly, are distinctly less dangerous than long-range weapons.

In training, we actually only rarely throw over distances of more than 10 meters (33 ft.). Usually I train with my knives over distances of 3–7 meters (10–23 ft.) because my garden allows distances of only up to 8 meters (26 ft.). This in turn reveals how small the dangers of sportive knife throwing actually are, and quite limits our safety aspects. For this reason you have exactly two possibilities for choosing a place for training:

1. You are in a spacious area that allows you to see any arriving person from afar, and thus you can't be surprised during training.

Sturdy shoes are generally recommended for knife throwing.

2. As an alternative solution, you have a fenced-in area at your disposal, meaning that behind your target disk there is nothing but a thick and high wall, a timber fence, or something similar.

Basic safety criteria are actually determined by our common sense. Nevertheless, for the sake of completeness, I want to point out the essential aspects here without drifting into banality if possible. Absolutely important: nobody is allowed to be behind, in front of, or directly next to the target, because an old German saying states: "A dagger in your back really puts you on the rack!"

In case you are training as a duo or with several other people at targets close to each other, always throw simultaneously and of course pick up the knives at the same time. Nobody should ever walk over to the target disk alone while his or her training partner finishes their series of throws in direct vicinity!

Nobody can be allowed to stand directly behind the thrower, because the semicircular striking movement often requires more space than estimated. This is especially important when you are being filmed by a partner to analyze your training. Especially long tomahawks are suitable for neatly ruining your training partner's lens, smartphone, or tablet in case he or she is too close behind your back while you are swinging backward for your powerful throw.

Children and adolescents are logically allowed to train only under the supervision—or at least with the consent—of an adult. They sometimes don't actually realize the dangers of a thrown knife to their surroundings. But even this ought to be obvious.

Also take care that the trajectory is completely clear and not blocked by dangling branches, bushes, or similar items, because ricochets with a heavy throwing knife are not free from danger. Every thrower ought to wear sturdy shoes, because a bouncing knife generally follows a totally uncontrolled trajectory for which the final place of impact can never be predicted. Hence you had better leave your trekking sandals and flip-flops at home—apart from the fact that you don't have a firm stance with such footwear anyway.

It is generally also not wrong to have a first-aid kit around for overall safety, just in case.

And although it is basically self-evident, here (once more) I emphasize that you never throw toward humans or animals—not even jokingly and not even pretending—because in just such a case the knife may inadvertently slip out of your hand!

This, in principle, is all there is with respect to the topic of safety during training. As said before, almost all aspects are actually self-evident and result from thinking logically.

5 The Short Whiplash Throw

When the basic exercise works well, we can now switch to another preparatory exercise that is executed in almost the same way but needs a bit more courage. Don't start this unless you have mastered the previous exercise—throwing at the target in front of you by means of a whiplash throw—at least about fifty times without any failure.

1. Instead of throwing at a lying target as before, you now stand in front an erected target that you constructed in the meantime according to your personal preferences.

2. Stretch your arm with the knife and stand in front of the target disk at a distance of 3 feet, counting from the tip of your shoes. Now, with outstretched arm, the knife will be about 1½ feet away from your target. Caution: hammer grippers widen the distance by an additional 12 to 20 inches.

3. Now you simply do the same as before: an aimed "Indiana Jones" whiplash move in the direction of your throwing target, followed by instinctively letting go of the knife as you did before. The entire action ought to be as dauntlessly, courageously, determinedly, and consistently made as possible. And always keep in mind: the more courageously, relaxed, and at the same time determinedly you are throwing, the less probable is a failure and the bouncing back of the knife linked to this.

You should now be able to perform this exercise without any problems, as long as you don't have problems with getting over your inner fear of the possible bouncing knife. Don't be afraid, and stay cool—you will succeed! After you let go of the knife, it will again make a bit less than a quarter turn and end up sticking in the disk.

And now a little tip that you ought to internalize from the very beginning: you can give your throws an additional "kick" of force by supporting the throw directly through breathing correctly. Maybe you are already doing this automatically by breathing out briefly and sharply at the moment you let go of the knife, as martial artists or boxers do when hitting or pushing. You surely know this from various everyday situations when trying to lift a heavy object. At the beginning this may not work very well, but when forcefully breathing out, you suddenly are able to lift that bag of concrete. So you are indeed able to increase your muscle force by using your so-called "breathing force" (the Japanese call this force *ki*; the Chinese call it *chi*). For us throwers, this is a little "boost" we can use profitably.

Also of elementary importance for sustainable (in the very sense of the word) and successful training: when letting go of the knife, your arm automatically makes a semicircular movement. Please continue this movement even after you have already let go of the knife. Among other things, you can watch this when looking at athletic spear throwers. This continuation of the throw is called "follow through." Many sources of mistakes can be eliminated if you focus on following through until it happens totally automatically at some point in time. In the end, only by following through can a controlled throwing movement and thus a consistently constant rotational speed of your throwing knives be achieved.

Even with this preparatory exercise it is of additional advantage for you if, after a few rounds, you select individual spots you want to aim at and hit, even if this is just to avoid knives colliding with each other.

When you have done this exercise several times in a row, after a short time you will reach a point at which this movement again feels natural, fluid, pleasant, and right. As soon as this is the case—maybe after ten rounds with three throws each—you are ready for our basic throw from a short distance of 10 feet.

The throwing line should be marked visibly, here for the 10-foot throw.

Letting go occurs very early, almost above the thrower's head.

53

6 The Basic Throw

Using a tape measure, measure off a distance of 10 feet, starting at the throwing target. Mark this point on the ground either with chalk, a piece of wood, or tape. My British thrower friend "Little" John Taylor—a 6½-foot-tall giant of Yorkshire—once used an earthworm as a "distance marker" but realized that his mark slowly and steadily moved, so this has proven not to be an ideal solution. Personally, I prefer a wooden board, which has a similar function as the springboard for broad jumps and immediately registers any violation.

The following basic throw from a short distance will be the basis of all further sportive knife throws on which everything that follows is based. In addition, the 10-foot distance is the shortest distance with a knife in official national and international contests.

Now put your front foot (the left or the right) at the distance mark in such a way that your shoe tip doesn't touch the mark—this means you may as well stay two inches behind it. Now you perform the same whipping, throwing movement as before with your throwing arm while instinctively aiming at the center of your target disk. Then just let go of the knife in the same instinctive way.

By the way, the objectively visible time of letting go is often judged totally wrong by the thrower. Many throwers think that they let go of the knife just at the moment the throwing hand points forward in the direction of the target, but this is not true. If this were the case, the knife would land in the ground directly in front of the thrower.

Well, this is interesting. But it doesn't make sense to think about this during training, because actually this movement from the very beginning happens more or less automatically—unless you have never thrown any kind of object at all in your entire life. In the best case, after you let go of the knife, it just makes another full turn and then sticks in your target, tip first. At this point it is not very important where exactly it sticks or how "neat" it looks, because here the main issue is that it sticks at all.

More-accurate aiming and focusing, and finally also hitting smaller targets, are developed only in the course of the following days, weeks, months, and even years of trying and training. Knife throwing is not something that can be learned online or in a correspondence course, because it has to be tested time and again and has to be felt in the real sense of the word. And this works only outdoors in fresh air, and in practice.

In case it did work, congratulations! And even if out of three thrown knives, only a single one sticks, this is still a noteworthy success, because in this case you verifiably did it right once. In the future, you just do it right more and more often, until eventually almost nothing can go wrong anymore. The way to this point is simply called "training."

In case throwing didn't work out according to your wishes and to your satisfaction, at this point we come to another important and actually elementary aspect of our sport: error analysis.

7 Error Analysis: Analyzing Failures and Correction

Trial and Error

Trial and error will faithfully be at your side as permanent teachers during further training; this I can promise you. Our kind of sport is highly demanding technically and not easy to learn—even though the results of advanced and longtime throwers quite often look so easy and playful. This apparent ease exhibited by experienced throwers may at the beginning be quite frustrating for the person in training. Please, don't let yourself be scared off or slowed down by this, because knife throwing is a delicate sport requiring fine motor skills and has very high demands on coordinative abilities. I always like to describe knife throwing as a mixture of martial arts, sportive shooting, juggling, and meditation.

In case you are annoyed about quite a few misses at the beginning, think about this for reassurance: during my career, I surely have had at least a hundred times more misses than you have had throwing attempts so far. You will grow only by means of your own mistakes, self-critical error analysis, and effective corrections. In the beginning, misses are just part of the sport, and luckily the knives don't suffer much from them.

While an archer after launching the arrow doesn't have to think much about whether the arrow will really stick in the target with its tip

In the end, another little tip to try as part of the process of training during your first attempts to throw from a short distance is to slowly and steadily increase the automatic nature of your motion sequence, since your throwing movements during the first fifty tries will become more and more fluid and relaxed. In the ideal case, everything will go very smoothly after some time of training. This kind of "becoming relaxed" can lead to instinctively speeding up the rotation of your knives, which in turn means that you can again decrease your distance from the target by a few inches.

ERROR SOURCE 2

Maybe you belong to the hammer grippers, who instinctively and right from the beginning, without being told to do so, put their thumb on the handle's back instead of putting it at the handle's side.

As already mentioned, knife throwing is a rather "outlaw" type of sport, and if you feel comfortable with this grip variant, then feel free to stay with it. No guideline, no paragraph, and no law of the thrower's world decrees that we must hold our knives only in a specific way. Many sport throwers I know who are very successful swear by the hammer grip technique, but they don't get around the principles described in the first passage of chapter 2.

The resting thumb is a strong "counterbearing" to the throw's rotation, and, during the process of launching the knife from your hand, this counterbearing in connection with the almost immovable and arrested wrist immensely slows down the rotational speed. Sometimes I throw with this technique for fun and the joy of experimenting, although I actually prefer the side pinch (i.e., gripping the knife with the thumb at the side). But in this case I have to extend the short distance by about 30 inches and thus have to throw from a distance of 12½ feet to perform a successful throw with just a single

61

revolution. In my opinion this is a disadvantage, because in competition I would give away precious distance by voluntarily moving away from the target a good deal without being required to do so.

The hammer grip—in case you feel comfortable with it—is of advantage as soon as you are able to throw over larger distances after more training. As soon as you have mastered this technique reliably, you are able to cover 16½ feet with a long throw with one rotation and 23 feet with two rotations. Fewer rotations also mean—in a quite simplified view—a reduction of possible sources for errors, meaning that advanced hammer grippers sooner or later will start to throw with only half a rotation from a distance of 10 feet.

Another small disadvantage of this way of positioning the thumb may result—in rare cases—in small "imbalances" during launch. If my thumb presses too strongly against the handle's left or right side while letting go of the knife, this results in "screw spins," as with high diving from a 10-meter platform. In this case the knives turn around their longitudinal axis and may stick in the target in a rather chaotic way.

Tilted Sticking in the Target

In principle, this is not bad as long as the knife sticks in the target tip first. But in case you want to make a correction here for "cosmetic" reasons, the slight malposition may be caused by one of the following:

1. Maybe the cause is the just-mentioned effect of a slightly unbalanced thumb during the hammer grip throw. If you want to correct this unbalance, you only have to feel during training how you can better center your resting thumb. After a few rounds you basically should be able to eliminate the flaw when focusing on it. Here it may also be helpful to grip the knife handle farther toward its end so that it can glide out of your hand easier. Then, in turn, it will rotate a bit faster.

Again, a throw that counts but is not technically correct: the knife doesn't stick in the target vertically, but obliquely.

2. A second possible cause may be that you move your elbow too far outward while swinging backward and then your arm gets into a kind of wobbly movement during launch. This in turn may have as a direct effect that your throwing hand is tilted, and this small deviation is transferred to the thrown weapon. In the end, your knife will stick in the disk somewhat skewed and twisted. In this case the correction is to reel your elbow in and focus on a forward stabbing, whipping movement directly past your head.

Complete Misses

Every now and then there are complete misses that neither stick in nor hit the target disk at all. They accompany every advanced thrower like good, old, somewhat annoying acquaintances who drop by every once in a while—quite probably without being asked to, at the most inapt times and without any invitation. But we are humans and not machines, and this means that every sport thrower always works on reducing the risk of misses by instinctive repetition of their movements. Nevertheless, the potential danger can't be eliminated completely—not even within the absolute world-class competitors.

If you have just started to throw knives, this part of your training practice quite often results in a test of your personal limits of frustration. Especially in the initial phase, the misses can quickly get on your nerves and, in the worst case, demoralize you. But here the following is important for you to recognize: you will quickly realize that it is of great advantage to train with a positive, relaxed, and quiet mind. Lay people often think that they ought to tackle training with a kind of "healthy aggression," but the opposite is the case.

Aggression and tension may make your throws more powerful, but quite often this is at the expense of required precision and may regularly lead to misses. Your training should instead take place at a time when you are "in a good mood," had a good day, or were successful with something. You especially ought to learn to be more indulgent with yourself and your achievements during the first twenty minutes of training, during the classic warming-up phase. Within this necessary time span, the sequence of movements for successful knife throws first has to consolidate and become automatic.

You are well advised not to let the distance to the target become too large during this time. A 100-meter sprinter doesn't immediately go to the starting block without warming up first before trying to achieve his or her personal minimum time. In the course of the brief warming up, you will slowly realize how the required movements become more and more pleasant, natural, and self-evident. Even if, in the course of your series of three throws each, you have one or two misses every now and then, your training is still successful. After all, you also have regularly recurring hits that you can be proud of.

This fact leads to the logical conclusion that you already can throw well in particular cases and know how it is done. All else is called automation, meaning that after a certain amount of training practice, your mistakes during the basic throw from a distance of 10 feet will become increasingly rare. And at some point you will very probably throw for half an hour, sip your coffee every once in a while, and then realize with astonishment that your knife not even once dropped to the ground.

If you already want to dive into root cause analysis right at the beginning of your career as a knife thrower, here once again are the most-important basic points:

1. Is your distance still correct? Perhaps you have to adjust the distance to the target and change your position. For this, check once again the passages about how to correct throws with over- or underrotation. To do an unambiguous error analysis, best let a training partner film you or film yourself during training. This way you are much better able to determine whether your knives rotate too fast or whether they don't have enough angular momentum. Subsequently you can adjust your technique or the distance to the target in accordance with the results. By means of recordings, you are able to more easily see, recognize, and eliminate errors, especially in your sequence of movements. In the course of your training, throws will usually also become ever more fluid and relaxed. According to experience, this means that you will be able to again gradually reduce the distance somewhat.

2. Do you still throw powerfully enough? When training together with newbies, I often experience that they have to overcome a certain timidness when throwing

a knife. For most people it is not a problem to throw balls, stones, or a Frisbee, but as soon as a "novice" holds a knife in his or her hands they instinctively feel somewhat uncomfortable. Quite often this is a simple matter of education ("knife, fork, scissors, flames have no place in children's games") that has to be totally overcome for our sport. Our throwing knives are no more than sport utensils. Please always throw courageously, without hesitation and with the proper momentum. During training, if possible, think less about the item you are holding in your hand and more about the target and the point on the disk you want to hit. This will surely be of help to you. At the beginning you can also make some test throws with a rubber ball or tennis ball, or in a pinch even with stones to get familiar with throwing at a target before you start using knives for this.

3. Is your throwing move still "round" and fluid? Do you still focus on the important "follow through" and the semicircular movement of the throwing arm?

These are the initial and purely technical aspects you have to take into account during the course of your training to make rapid process. Later I'll also talk a bit about the nontechnical—the mental—criteria, because these factors are almost even more decisive.

8   Position and Stance

If you want to learn how to defeat your opponent, you first have to learn to stand stable.

—*Gichin Funakoshi, founder of modern karate*

Normal Foot Position

At this point I once again come back to the proverbial "lawlessness" of our sport. What's valid for holding our knives is also valid for our basic position for throwing. This simply means there is no general rule for a thrower's stance. But there is a statistical value with respect to which stance a large number of sport throwers prefer. This means concretely that sport throwers usually stand with their left foot forward, implying that as a right-handed person (lefties do it exactly the opposite) you stand in a more or less low, loose, and relaxed lunge position with your left foot in front.

Usually this happens totally automatically, without the thrower consciously deciding on it. This foot position during launch is also normal with athletic throwing disciplines. The advantage is in the transmission of force by sharply turning the hip and shoulder inward during the process of throwing. If you want to throw a stone as far as possible into a river, you will very probably also automatically throw from this position. Roughly estimated, about 85 percent of all sport throwers launch from this position.

Other Foot Positions

Right Leg in Front

I personally can present more-exotic foot positions at this point, because one of them is my favorite contest and throwing position. In contrast to the above-described position, as a right-handed person I have my right foot in front. But this also has disadvantages, which I won't hold back. Of course, in this position I am unable to give the throw as much force of the entire body, because the sharp momentum of hip and shoulder is missing completely. This lack I have to fill with additional work by the triceps and pectorals.

Whether this may or may not work effectively was already tested in the TV show *Galileo* (broadcast by the German TV channel ProSieben) in 2007, when, by means of a high-speed camera, the velocity of my flying knives was determined to be close to 34 miles per hour. Even powerful throwers who stand in a conventional way with the left foot in front rarely throw faster than about 37 miles per hour in the course of normal training and during contests. In any case, my throwing arm has to perform more work than theirs.

As a karate sportsman I can point out some parallels to the budo sport, because in traditional karate there is also the straight fist punch forward, the *oi-zuki*, while stepping forward. Here the pushing fist is also positioned over the foot in front. Thus the karate combatant for a short period becomes someone with an "ambling gait"—which at least at the beginning is felt to be an unnatural movement and in any case needs a certain amount of time to become familiar with.

Last but not least, in sword fights as well as in fencing this position is an important prerequisite for sustaining one's own health. When striking with a sword in the right hand, it is mandatory that the right foot is also in front, because otherwise the sword combatant hits his

Foot position: standing in a casual lunge stance, depending on the thrower's preferences. Correspondingly, left-handed people prefer having the right foot in front, while right-handers prefer having the left foot forward.

or her own left knee if the sword misses the target. Similarly, a fencer always holds their thrusting hand over the knee of the same body half to more quickly bridge the distance to the opponent by means of a deep lunge.

But where is the advantage of the "inverted" foot position in knife throwing? With my position it is easier to keep the right shoulder more exact and straighter in line with the target line, and thus I have an instrument at hand that facilitates aiming. This means I simply throw more precisely under these circumstances. Although I am also able to throw from the conventional position, making my throws a bit more powerful, this also results in them being more imprecise. I also stand stably and my rear foot is always "glued" to the ground. But this is a pure matter of taste and not a rule that is valid for everybody.

Cowboy Stance

Even further from standard is the cowboy stance, preferred by throwers of the Czech Republic. As with a cowboy during a duel with pistols, the legs are held parallel in a casual way, similar to a kind of constricted rider's stance on the ground. Thus the thrower's body is facing the

The cowboy stance: legs apart with the feet almost parallel. Their distance is (depending on body size) about half a leg's length apart.

Czech Stanislav "Stany" Havel (*at right*, with Andy Fisher) always throws from a "cowboy stance." At Callac (Bretagne) in August 2014, he hit the target with a tomahawk from a distance of more than 88½ feet, setting a new world record for distance.

target head-on. Throws are set in motion with a slight bow tension of the upper torso and are augmented by the thrower's back bending backward a bit while striking out and then hurling it forward during launch by straining the abdominal muscles. I don't have any explanation why this stance is especially popular in the Czech Republic, but I can confirm that the Czechs have an excellent team of throwers at world-class level who in 2014 won the world championship in the team contests. Almost all contestants of the Czech Republic throw like cowboys, so it seems to work well to "fire" aimed and successful throws from this unusual position.

9 Further Development of Your Training

If you have already dealt with our basic throw from a distance of 10 feet for a while, you'll probably soon arrive at the point of advanced automation of your throws. This means you'll have increasingly fewer misses, very probably already focus on the target disk's center, and also have increasingly better hits. At this point I can invite you to pause for a moment and be satisfied with your achievements. After just a few days of trying the right throwing movements and feeling the required technical sequence, you have very probably reliably mastered throwing from a short distance. Maybe it already works so well that you are able to make about thirty throws without the knife "ringing" and falling to the ground?

Then you can "gear up another notch." When throwing knives you will now realize a fundamental law if you already hit well and reliably from a distance of 10 feet: every additional rotation of your thrown knife means about 6½ feet more in distance—assuming that you also throw using the side pinch. In case you now ask yourself why the first revolution of your throw needs 10 feet, it's simply because it is more than a single turn. In fact this is a one and a quarter rotation, because as a thrower you already let go of the knife when it was almost above your head.

This law of an additional 6½ feet per knife rotation naturally is valid only if you always throw in the same way, because in the long run this is the goal in training and the reason for our success. Just the automation of your movements produces hardly any deviations in the motion sequence when comparing throws, and this is what we are aiming for!

After warming up by throwing from a short distance, simply move 6½ feet backward, resulting in you being 16½ feet away from the target. Seen from this point, your target already looks quite small, doesn't it?

Don't be shy: simply throw the knife toward the target in the same way you successfully did before from a distance of 10 feet. You will realize that the knife makes a second revolution and then sticks in the wood again. If not the first knife, then surely one in the series.

You will further notice that this increased distance is not as forgiving with respect to technical errors as is the short distance. The effect of a slight error in movement is multiplied and expounded by increasing the distance. Thus here the same tip as at the beginning: please be patient with your progress, because the 16½-foot throw is already a ballpark for advanced throwers and requires a good deal more training than the short 10-foot distance.

In case you have two or more series of complete failures in a row with the new, longer distance, it makes sense to go back to the short distance every once in a while and to train some more rounds from this position. You will be astonished by how easy throwing from 10 feet suddenly will be for you. Thereafter, when you are back "in step" again, you may well go back to 16½ feet—probably with more success. When proceeding in this way you can easily recognize through practice the setup of sportive knife throwing: from near to far, from large to small targets, and from easy to demanding and difficult.

As previously mentioned briefly, during the standard contests in our competitions the distance may be increased even farther by also throwing from 23 feet. In our training this requires an additional rotation of the thrown knife. From this distance you have to throw the knife in such a way that, after launch, it will rotate in the air three times. In addition, you will realize that from this distance not only does the 4-inch bull's eye looks pretty small, but the entire target disk does!

Some overly motivated beginners who start with this royal discipline too early and without reasonable development sometimes even miss the target disk completely. This once again leads us back to the rule that sportive knife throwing lives by methodical and systematic training and by being built up over the long run. If you progress to long distances too soon and too impatiently, your training will quickly mutate into a "wild flinging" with a hit rate of maybe 30 percent, and you have to avoid this to not become frustrated unnecessarily.

In addition, I want to remark that this "6½ feet per rotation" rule can't be continued indefinitely, because the farther you move away from the disk, the higher the ballistic trajectory of your knife becomes. Greetings from gravity! At some point—for me this starts at about 42½ feet—you have to use part of your force just for the task of providing more altitude to the trajectory of your knife. But more altitude also means the knife has to bridge a larger distance to the target. For extended distances, the unit in feet on the ground measuring the space needed for one rotation of the knife slowly decreases with the distance.

I once again want to remind you of my tip to be patient and indulgent with yourself. Nobody stands behind you with a whip in hand! To mention precise numbers: with every beginner, throwing from a distance of 16½ feet demands at least two months up to half a year of preparation and training until a certain consistency of successful throws can be seen. You, too, will need your time, but it pays off!

10 Alternate Grip Variants

Knife throwing is an extremely versatile and multifaceted kind of sport. This can be seen in the diverse possibilities of holding a knife prior to launch. You already know two different variants of holding your knife before throwing it: the side pinch and the hammer grip. The basic difference between the two is the position of your thumb on the knife handle's backside with the hammer grip, resulting in a distinct slowdown of the rotational speed. Additionally, there is the turn of your hand through almost 90 degrees. Apart from this there are other variations, but these can be deduced from the fact that some knife models hardly allow any other technique.

The "Pinch" Grip

The pinch grip is another of the "classics" you might have already seen. Some knives are so small that you may want to grab them only between your thumb and the joint of your index finger. This technique not only is very energy sapping but also leads to knife rotations that are so fast that they can hardly be controlled.

In September 2007 I was asked by the *Galileo* show of the TV channel ProSieben to throw small steak knives, carpenter nails, and

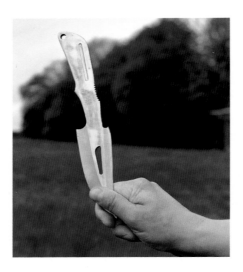

The "pinch grip" is a classic way of holding a knife and is especially used with small knives. Take care of your fingers in case the blade is sharpened.

screwdrivers, among other things, to make the show somewhat more colorful for viewers; out of necessity I had to throw these items by means of the pinch grip. I did not see any other option, but luckily this worked out well.

The "Clamp" Grip

Whoever doesn't like the pinch grip as an alternative can use the "clamp" grip, also called the "horizontal blade" grip. This is especially well suited for light blades and preferably for knives with a sharp edge, or knives whose edge is sharpened on both sides, as is often the case with combat knives or "tactical knives."

Here the risk of injuring your hand is excluded, but training this type of throw is not easy. This kind of grip, with its specific way of resting the thumb, leads to a significant slowdown of the knife's rotational speed. With a bit of training you may be able to decrease the turns of the knife to such an extent that at some time you will be able to throw a shorter knife from a distance of 16½ feet with just half a rotation.

Throwing this way takes a lot of exertion of back and shoulder and is not primarily done by a movement of the elbow. The knives hit the target with high speed but often stick in the wood in a somewhat chaotic manner because, during the short flight, they inevitably spin around their longitudinal axis. The reason for this is that with this technique, you throw the knife with its side surface facing forward and not just with the slim knife back.

According to the laws of aerodynamics, a flying body tries to find the position with the least drag and thus starts to spin around its longitudinal axis. This, too, is a reason why the clamp grip is suitable mainly for throwing over short distances. For me personally, together

The "clamp grip" is also called the "horizontal blade grip" and is especially suited for light throwing knives that also have one or two sharp blade edges.

with the purely aesthetic aspect, the accuracy of aiming is also diminished, so I don't want to use this technique in competitions. Nevertheless, it is interesting to know that this kind of technique exists.

The "Wild West" Blade Throw

In case you are a western fan, you perhaps remember that the heroes of Wild West movies almost exclusively hold their knives by the blade when throwing. This kind of throwing I found extremely fascinating as an adolescent, especially since it looked somewhat "cool." From today's point of view, the reason for the blade throw is easy to understand for utility knives: the handles of utility knives are often constructed ergonomically, with a finger guard or cross guard, as well as a pommel to prevent your hand from slipping. These parts make working with these knives easier but at the same time make launching the knife from the handle more difficult. On the other hand, the blade edges of these knives are usually ground to be very sharp, so I want to mention some specifics with respect to throwing them. After all, we don't want to unnecessarily turn into wholesale purchasers of Band-Aids.

To start training on blade throws, it is recommended to first throw with blunt throwing knives (such as the "Pro-Balance Thrower"), or with knives whose blades are not sharpened. At the same time I advise against using the hammer grip for the blade throw, because employing this technique will avoid hand injuries only when you're using a totally blunt knife for throwing.

But one thing is clear: as soon as the thrower wants to throw a sharp knife this way, he or she will inevitably cut their thumb or the inside of other fingers. It doesn't matter at all in which way the thrower grabs the knife at the blade, since an injury is almost preprogrammed. Hence, please exclude this technique from your training and use the pinch grip, if possible, with the thumb resting at the blade's side.

Since you already know about the mutual dependence of distance and knife rotation, you can make your life a bit easier for the moment: for initially testing the blade throw, stand only 6½ feet from the target, meaning your knife has to do only about half a rotation.

You have already mastered the basic throw quite well; hence, throwing from a shorter distance is surely a trifle for you. But here the following technical aspect is important to still be able to throw knives with a sharp edge the same way in the future: always take care to hold the knife straight during launch, with the sharp edge facing outward, and never toward the palm of your hand!

If you do this wrong, the launch and the initial starting rotation of the knife easily lead to a cut on your hand. Also this way the knife will turn itself into the "right position," meaning the blunt back faces forward, as is the case with the throw with one rotation.

All this you can try out delightfully without any danger, by using a blunt throwing knife until you automatically do it right without having to think about it. During launch it is especially important to open your fingers during the flow of moves to avoid the sharp blade edge in case of a mishap.

With the "Wild West" blade throw, the launch can also best be described as letting the blade glide out of your hand. In principle this works according to the same rules as the usual throw with your hand on the knife's handle. Try this from a distance of 6½ feet and you will surely immediately be successful. What you are able to do from a distance of 10 feet should not be any problem at all for you from a distance of 6½ feet.

Everything described in this section of the chapter so far is only a preliminary exercise for things to come: the "Wild West" throw from a distance of 13 feet! For this you move about 3 feet behind your 10-foot marker and then throw the knife in exactly the same way as in the preliminary exercise, but now with an additional full rotation. The knife now rotates one and three-quarter times, but we throwers always round down, so we name this throw "1½ spin."

This new throwing variant will also be a lot of joy for you after some tries. It is also of a certain relevance to train this variant, because in case you ever want to participate in an official contest, the so-called walk-back is of significance in the finals. "Walk-back" means here that a thrower doesn't stay at a certain distance but after three successful throws has to walk back to the next distance farther away from the target.

For example, after three throws from a distance of 10 feet there immediately follow three more throws from a distance of 13 feet to

For "Wild West" throws, injuries of the throwing hand are almost preprogrammed because of the sharpened blade edge—regardless of which way the thrower holds the knife. Best to train with blunt, nonsharpened blades.

the target. Then the thrower has to move farther back to 16½ feet, 20 feet, and 23 feet. The walk-back is an extremely demanding task for the thrower and requires a high degree of experience, training, skill, and flexibility (more about this later in chapter 24, about contests and their rules).

The "No Spin" Grip

This throwing and grip variant is linked to a very interesting throwing technique. Especially within the school of Russian and Asian throwers, decades ago there were thoughts about whether it is possible to throw a knife in such a way that it doesn't rotate during flight, and this way one may be able to be totally independent of distance measurements.

"Instinctive throwing" was called into being—the "no spin" technique (= no rotation). But how is this supposed to work at all? As we know, the lever relations of the human body inevitably lead to the knife's rotation after launch; sometimes slow, sometimes faster. How can this rotation be avoided?

Short answer: it can't be avoided completely, because in the end the knife still turns, but it turns extremely slowly. As you already know from the hammer grip technique, the thrower needs a kind of counterbearing during launch to slow down the rotation. With the hammer grip, this counterbearing is the thumb resting on the backside of the knife's handle, and thus the knife rotates slower and more sluggishly in the air.

This counterbearing principle with the "no spin" technique is virtually carried to its extremes, because here the index finger is put down in a similar way—but now on the knife handle's top side. Swinging the knife backward takes place with the ball of your hand facing forward and with a very flexible wrist that gets totally blocked at launch. As soon as the knife's rotation is about to start, the "index finger action" takes over and provides an effective countermeasure by means of a "backspin," which implies that counterpressure is acting on the knife handle while you let go of the knife.

If you ever tried to throw a flat stone in such a way that it skips on the surface of a lake several times, you automatically exerted a comparable backspin on the stone by means of your snapping wrist and via your index finger. In this way the initiated knife rotation is countered to such an extent that some well-trained "no-spinners" are able to throw their knives from a distance of more than 33 feet practically without any rotation. With this throwing technique the knife's rotation always struggles against the backspin caused by one's index finger.

The "no spin" grip doesn't cause any rotation of the knife and makes the throw independent of any distance, but the technique is complicated and hard to learn.

82

This looks very impressive with masters of this skill, but I don't want to hide the fact that this skill not only is extremely difficult to learn but also needs a very high amount of training. Even experienced contest sport throwers (and I don't exclude myself from this!) may sometimes almost become despaired when training this throwing technique.

In the overall-precision competitions of international contests, so far only a single sport thrower has participated with this technique. One reason may be that this throwing variant is a bit less precise with respect to aiming than the usual rotational throwing technique. This is comprehensible, because the index finger serving as a counterbearing may during launch inadvertently lead the knife in an unwanted direction. Besides that, the important and stabilizing kinetic energy of the rotation is missing.

In this context I would like to remark that "no spin" doesn't work equally well with any knife. For example, my competition knives have a weight of 21½ ounces each at an overall length of 15 inches. These can't be slowed down by any index finger at the moment of launch. Suitable for no-spin throwing are especially smaller knives with a length of about 10 to 11 inches.

Meanwhile, a kind of "no-spin hype" has started—apart from actual competitions—which I don't share. For aesthetic reasons I already like it when my knives rotate in the air like a boomerang and then stick in the target tip first as if by magic.

Besides that, with many throwers of this discipline the "no spin" trajectory of thrown weapons often looks quite chaotic, because the knives frequently flutter or rotate around their longitudinal axes but only rarely fly straight forward like an arrow. This is caused by the lack of kinetic rotational energy, which stabilizes the trajectory of conventional throws with rotation. Another reason is that a knife doesn't have any aerodynamic characteristics, in contrast to a dart, crossbow arrow, or spear.

Last but not least, I don't really like the designs, shapes, and looks of most "no spin" knives. They rather remind me of a dentist's tools, tent stakes, and scalpels. But this is also a question of individual taste.

Nevertheless, the "no spin" technique in any case is a very interesting facet of knife throwing and another instance of "to each his own." There is no "right" or "wrong" here, but rather a "one way or the other." In any case, I wish you much joy with trying and especially lots of patience. You will need it!

Russian Yuri Fedin (who unfortunately died much too early in spring 2015) took "no spin" to a certain perfection I ungrudgingly concede. His teaching videos about the "Fedin style" can still be admired on the internet, and thus Yuri is immortal at least in this way. There are also a couple of excellent "no-spinners" within the German and international communities of throwers whose tutorials in the internet are very well crafted and demonstrate the technique clearly.

In this context I have to add a few well-meaning words of warning I simply can't suppress. Some followers of the "no spin" technique like to mention a special and additional aspect as a "positive" argument for their style of throwing: "Throwing knives in this way turns throwing into a reliable tool for self-defense, since the distance to the opponent doesn't have any technical relevance anymore." Well, more about that in the next chapter.

Good throwing axes have a relatively short head with an edge of about 2–3 inches, as well as a straight shaft of hardwood.

Comparison: real throwing ax (*top*) with an edge of 2+ inches and a 19½-inch shaft and a hatchet unsuitable for accurate throwing (*below*).

again, even though the distance is only 13 feet in the beginning. But for throwing series with the ax, you have to take some small issues into account, which I will explain in more detail at a later point. Athletes skilled at crafts usually rework their axes individually or, in some cases, even forge them.

13 Throwing the Axe

About the Principles

The throwing weapons have to be such that they can be thrown with a single hand similar to knives. For contests the ax has to weigh at least 18 ounces. This is no big deal because even some knives weigh more. In addition, the blade edge can't be longer than 4¾ inches, which is already a quite generous measure. This limit exists to avoid a thrower using a hypothetical oversized blade somehow—with a bit of luck—to scratch the bull's eye in the center of the disk. This kind of "unfair competition" is thus excluded by the rules.

Historically seen, throwing axes are pure weapons of war that in former times were feared by every opponent as throwing weapons, as well as in direct close combat, and rightfully so. The early medieval Franks created a design of their own for throwing axes called "Francisca," with which they spread fear among their opponents.

The "Francisca" was designed as a weapon purely meant for throwing and close combat. Today it can still be found among some athletes participating in contests. In earlier times it was suitable for smashing the shields of opponents on the battlefield—of course, the same could be done to other items or body parts! To this end, the ax was forcefully and vertically thrown by warriors in the direction of the opponent but sometimes was also thrown horizontally just slightly above the ground. This way the ax flew toward the enemy while rotating in an unpredictable, sometimes even jumping manner, hitting the enemy's legs.

In contrast, the war axes of North American natives—the tomahawks—generally had a very slim edge without an elaborate tip at their heads. The backside of the ax head often had an individual design and was more or less large and massive. The Indian ax is my preferred tool for ax throwing. The legendary war ax is nicely shaped, not too heavy (21 ounces), and in addition plain, without frills and functional. From my experience in competitions, I know that our flying throwing axes and tomahawks are especially popular among viewers because laypeople presume an enhancement of the art in comparison to knife throwing.

But this is not the case (but don't tell this to anybody!). Ax throwing is actually easier than throwing knives as soon as you have become accustomed to a special detail: the center of gravity of a throwing ax.

The Center of Gravity

In contrast to throwing knives, with their center of gravity more or less in the center of the knife's body, the center of gravity for a throwing ax is always far from the ax's center—it's a little bit in front of the ax head. This is logical, because the steel ax head weighs a good deal more than the wooden handle. For our sport this aspect is not really important, because the ax is always thrown from the handle's end—holding the handle—and you never throw from the blade.

Reconstruction of a "Francisca"

Finding the center of gravity of a throwing ax

But in case you try to throw an ax for the first time toward the target after exclusively dealing with knife throwing for some time, it may happen that the new, unfamiliar center of gravity of the ax plays a little trick on you. The center of gravity makes the ax glide out of your hand a little too high, because the heavy ax head "pulls" the ax upward at the moment of release by means of the circular movement of swinging your arm. Looking back at my first experiences with tomahawks, I have to admit that at the beginning of my training, the axes often flew in a generous arc right over the target disks.

On the other hand, throwing axes is made much easier by the inertia of the throwing weapons in the air. After getting used to "letting go of the hawks" just a whiff of a tenth of one second later, your axes will provide a lot of joy for you: they can be thrown much more consistently!

This inertia simply results from the larger dimensions and weight of a throwing ax, so the throw is much easier to control. Even larger distances can be managed reliably after a rather short amount of time. Indeed, these improvements happen quicker than with throwing knives.

14 Basic Training

With respect to learning how to throw axes, the basic exercise looks the same as the basic throw with knife throwing. Put a wooden target disk on the ground in front of you, then grab the ax handle at its end in a way that is comfortable for you; either the thumb is on top, at the handle's backside, or it is placed on the handle's side. Now go ahead!

At first, focus on a point on the disk, then make a movement as with chopping wood and just let go of the ax at the end of your arm's circular movement. The good piece has no other choice: it follows the laws of physics and moves in accordance with tangential centrifugal acceleration toward the target. During this, the ax performs the beginning of a short rotational movement and then sticks in the target wood.

You will also realize that this basic exercise is really very easy—almost as easy as chopping wood! After repeating the exercise a few times, you will have internalized the motion sequence and we can go on. Hence we won't dawdle around with interludes but will start directly with the basic throw from a short distance of 10 feet.

Still, be careful: throwing axes rotate a bit slower in the air. We stand at a distance of 13 feet for the short distance, because otherwise our throwing weapons would not have a chance to rotate even once. But don't bother unnecessarily, just try it out.

Of elementary importance: never throw several axes at a single disk! It is almost a natural law that if you hit the wooden handle of an

already sticking ax, you will art-
fully split it in half. This is extremely unfavorable when it
happens during training at a place
of competition and you have
neither a replacement handle nor
a replacement ax. Always throw
axes separately toward one target,
or alternatively throw each at a
different target.

The grip during a "normal" throw

During the basic throw onto a lying
target, we never change the distance,
because we would have to slow down
the rotation. The distance always stays
the same.

The basic throw is just for getting
accustomed to the ax.

Rotation: Taking aim and throwing is done in one flowing, rotating movement.

15 Some Material Science

At this point I want to remark that axes with conventional wooden handles always ought to be preferred over so-called "full tang" pieces. The latter are axes made from a single piece of flat steel. I would never choose one of the models of this construction type available on the market, because very probably they are not suited to my throwing style and my needs as a thrower. They can't be customized either, because steel is hard to process.

Tomahawks with wooden handles are mass produced, too, but these have the advantage that you are still able to modify handle length and customize the 'hawks in accordance with your individual needs. All throwers are individualists, and their throwing techniques differ considerably from each other. Tomahawks available on the market are usually delivered by factories with handles so long that they almost always have to be shortened.

After some trials you will discover that you will have to shorten the handle in accordance with your needs to successfully score a hit from 13 feet by means of a single rotation. This means—in case you need 14¾ feet of distance for a single rotation, using the ax with its initial handle length—at first saw off 2 inches from the handle and try again.

But with further shortening you have to be careful: once sawn off, the length is gone. Although you are able to glue the end piece back on, this is just patchwork, and you will have to put another $12 or so on the counter for a new hickory ax handle. The whole issue is a question of cautious trying and carefully approaching the right length to perform successful, well-aimed throws with your ax. Here, fine motor skills are required.

In this context you can well see that the ax's handle butt should always be straight. The quite often ergonomically shaped handles of many household and camping axes make throwing more difficult, similar to throwing utility knives. Although you have my blessings, if you borrow the household ax from your cellar for a start, you either ought to straighten the handle's butt prior to throwing or, as an alternative, exchange the complete handle.

If you buy a throwing ax, it is further recommended to saw off the wood shaft protruding at the top to about ¼ inch above the ax head. With a rotation of just slightly too much, this excess wood would hit the target disk first and cause an unnecessary, avoidable miss, because the tomahawk bounces off.

In addition, I advise you to also grind the sides of the blade directly behind the tip to some extent. A sufficient grind is ¾ inch, but this lets your axes stick in the target easier with the "reverse throw."

Throwing ax with a subsequently sharpened tip

99

16 The "Reverse" Ax Throw

This technique is a US invention and specialty that became a permanent part of European contests in 2014. You just learned and tried out the classic ax throw: you stand at a distance of 13 feet in front of the target and, after a successful throw, your thrown object sticks in the target with the ax handle pointing downward.

For the reverse throw, the thrower holds the ax differently during launch, in such a way that the ax's blade edge points at the thrower's face and the ax's backside points in the direction of the target. To make this throw work, the thrower has to walk backward for at least 3 feet and throw his or her ax from a distance of at least 16 feet with the same movements practiced before. In this way half a rotation is added to the throw. The result is that the ax sticks in the target again, but this time it is upside down: the ax handle points upward.

From experience I can say that this throwing variant feels very comfortable after a short period of getting accustomed to it. As soon as you have achieved some confidence at 13 feet, the reverse ax throw will probably be very easy for you, because it looks much more difficult than it actually is. Viewers always find this type of throw very amazing.

In the official finals of the world championship, throws from 5 meters (16.5 ft.) and 8 meters (26 ft.) are required, and the 5-meter throw is required to be "handle upward." But most throwers also perform the throw from a distance of 8 meters in this way. Logically this is done with an additional full rotation. In numbers, this means one and a half and two and a half rotations.

If for the throw you hold the ax in your hand reversely, . . .

. . .it will correspondingly stick in the target with its head facing downward.

101

17 Good Throwing Axes

Here the market is relatively clear, because the variety of available items in specialized shops is not as large for axes as it is with respect to throwing knives. As already mentioned, please ignore full-tang axes. They are quite expensive, often only marginally functional, and, in addition, quite frequently too small and too light to even be allowed in competitions.

Thus we reasonably restrict ourselves to classic axes with wooden handles. The best and at the same time cheapest throwing axes off the shelf at the moment, in my opinion, are those of the US company Cold Steel. All the models are quite affordable, stable, and very functional. Also the ax handles can be bought separately, in case you inadvertently "split" one during training or competition or ruin it by misses.

Especially the model "Trail Hawk" (21 ounces) is an excellent throwing ax, and my personal competition and world championship tomahawk. The hand-forged hunting hatchet of Gränsfors, Sweden (*see on right*), is actually not a throwing ax but an all-around tool that you can also use for cutting, chopping wood, and, because of its sharpness, gutting fish and field-dressing game. The hunting hatchet doesn't fly badly, but it is a quite precious one of its kind and I surely wouldn't allow everybody to throw it.

By the way, with the "Rifleman's Hawk" (*top right*) you can see especially well how far the wooden handle protrudes above the ax

Various throwing axes: at left is the hunter's hatchet by Gränsfors, in the center the "Rifleman's Hawk" with a weight of about 2¼ pounds, and at right the "Trailhawk," the author's preferred throwing ax (*top*). In the image on the right is the hand-forged "Norse Hawk" by Kari Salonius.

head when delivered from the factory. This means immediately clamp it into a vise and get rid of the excess wood!

At almost 2 pounds, the "Rifleman's Hawk" is surely not a dwarf and needs an above-average, forceful thrower's arm, but I actually do know some thrower friends who downright swear by this hawk regardless of the distance.

The model "Norse Hawk" is an excellent choice, especially when a thrower tends to throw with too much spin so that the ax hits the target disk at about a 45-degree angle. This way the tip of this hawk "bites" wonderfully into the wood. But in case you throw the same way I do, the design of this ax blade can quickly turn into a disadvantage. Thrown this way, the broad ax blade frequently bounces back, even though the tomahawk hits correctly with the blade facing forward. For this reason I parted with the Norse Hawk years ago. May it be of good service to another thrower!

The "Pipe Hawk" model is a very prettily shaped, classic Native American tomahawk. Although it has a pipe head on the backside of the ax head instead of a hammer surface, this is meant only as an ornament; you can't use it for smoking. This tomahawk is suitable only for strong throwers because it weighs 1¾ pounds and thus, like the "Rifleman's Hawk," is outside the lightweight class.

The hunter's hatchet by Gränsfors is delivered with a cover for the edge, as is the case with almost all utility axes. With throwing axes it is often missing after leaving the factory. You can either make one yourself or have a sheath maker do it.

18 Loose Fit: A Common Ax Disease

Every now and then, it may happen that the ax head loosens at the shaft. One cause can be exchanging the handle. This happens rather rarely because experience shows that exchange handles always fit accurately. Sometimes the handles are even a bit oversized, meaning you have to hammer the ax head into place with a few powerful blows. A tomahawk fitted in such a way doesn't get loose soon again.

Much more frequently it happens that ax handles become loose due to misses when throwing, as with inadvertently hitting the disk with the handle first. Because of the heavy ax head, there are enormous forces at work here that challenge the stability of the connection of ax head and shaft. In earlier times the tip was to put loose-fitting axes into water for a while prior to training or a contest, because the wood expands and thus the ax head sits firmly on the shaft again.

Even though this may work, I don't recommend this special recipe. I would like to give you an explanation for this:

1. Water is a natural enemy of steel. With your water trick you just cause your throwing axes to rust, especially on the inside of the ax head, which you can't reach with normal maintenance.

2. The ax heads of most models are attached to the wooden handle by means of a small headless screw so the heads receive additional stability. This screw

would also start to rust from the inside and seize up the steel thread of the ax. With this, you would run into problems in case you ever wanted to separate the ax head from its wooden shaft at a later time.

3. The wood of the handle would also suffer from watering in the long run. With drift wood at a beach, you can see very well what happens to wood that was in the water for too long: it leaches out and becomes brittle, dry, and porous. With this, its use as a handle or shaft for tools is inevitably obviated. And last but not least, watering is not a long-term solution because the wood dries up again after a short time, and the ax head is loose once more.

There is a much-simpler way to tackle the problem of loose ax heads that causes much less wear and needs only five minutes of your time:

Step 1: Unscrew the small headless screw in the ax body (if there is one).

Step 2: Drive the ax head down about 4 inches with a few well-dosed hammer blows (best with a material-friendly rubber mallet) so the upper part of the wooden shaft is freely accessible. This will be fairly easy, since the head was loose anyway.

Step 3: Wrap textile tape around the handle at exactly the spot where the ax head was before. If possible, don't let the tape overlap at its end but make it flush. Usually no more than one layer is required, because in case you wrap too much tape around the head, the ax head won't fit on top of it later.

Step 4: Move the ax head back to its original place by means of a few hammer blows onto the shaft's end. For this you don't even have to clamp the ax into a vise; you can even hold it with your hand.

Step 5: Tighten the headless screw once more. Because the tape is exactly underneath the screw, very probably it has a better fit than before, but if you want you can omit the screw altogether from now on.

This procedure is also recommended in case the screw gets lost at some point, the inside thread jams, or the screw can't be tightened anymore for other reasons. From my experience, the tomahawk will hold together very firmly for a long time. I have treated two of my competition tomahawks this way, and they fly in training and contests without any trouble and without wobbling at all, although the screws of both hawks have been missing for a couple of years.

Correct "taping" of a tomahawk is done within five minutes.

107

19 The Meditative Effect of Knife and Ax Throwing

Knife throwing is an ambivalent kind of sport. On the one hand, the process per se is more than just simple: you stand in front of your target disk and try to hit the target you are aiming at as precisely and exactly in the center as possible. There is almost nothing simpler than this! There are only you, your throwing weapon, and the target. Everything is in the "here and now."

On the other hand, it is not easy to learn the required motion sequence, and it takes time until you are able to recall it halfway automatically. And we sport throwers not only are confronted with the wish to hit the target but also from the very beginning have to deal with the physical basics and laws of rotating weapons.

From the multitude of demands a sport thrower has to meet, a high degree of the ability to focus necessarily results, paired with forbearance (toward your own mistakes) and a tough stamina, because you want to make progress and slowly become better. Conversely, this inevitably leads to your mind not having any thoughts about everyday issues during training. With this, knife and ax throwing meets many ideal requirements for so-called mindfulness meditation.

The Thrower Tunnel Vision

If you reduce the concept of meditation to the smallest common denominator, this action—expressed in a very simplified way—means nothing else than idleness in a very focused way. In our achievement-oriented culture of multitasking, this is extremely difficult for many people. Just at the very moment you try not to think about anything at all, thoughts come to your mind like swarms of locusts. But with some types of sports—including knife throwing—practice leads to the highest possible channeling of your own attention. During training, the athlete can think of almost nothing else but his or her throwing knives, the target they are aiming at, and the moves to be done. And what should be so special about that?

Let's make a brief comparison and take three athletes as examples: a marathon runner, a swimmer, and a soccer player. These three have lots of time during training, as well as during contests, for ruminating a lot: about the grades of their children at school, the shopping list for the weekend, planning a vacation, job projects, and so on. These can creep into the mind of a runner while he or she runs through the forest, or into the head of a swimmer while counting the tiles between the ninth and tenth swimming lanes, or might be the train of thought of a center forward in case he or she has to wait too long for a decisive pass to shoot a goal.

Knife throwers, in contrast, don't have their mind free for things like that. Focusing on only one or two essential items in mind after training usually leads to a kind of mental "refreshment," even though shoulders and arms hurt a bit. But even this we register only at the end of the day, not during training.

109

The elementary concentration in the "here and now" on only two essential points—the target and the technical performance of the throw—clears your head thoroughly. And with an advanced thrower, the automation of the motion sequence at some time leads to a point of freedom of your mind that reliably causes you to focus only on the target, while the movements themselves are automatically recalled.

This kind of felt freedom in the art of Zen is often called "emptiness," but this term can't be equated with lack of meaning or lack of content, but rather with "cleaning up your mind" and the conscious, attentive restriction to the essential. Throw out all the bulky waste of thoughts from the apartment of the compulsive hoarder of your mind; throw out all the irksome, unnecessary, and everyday monotony!

This law of the state of emptiness is also present in many Asian martial art systems, in which, by countless repetition of movements,

The tunnel vision of a thrower is symbolic of the concentration prior to throwing. While aiming at the target, the athlete performs the backswing and subsequent forward move totally automatically.

a "degree of freedom" should also be achieved where, as a person training, you don't have to think about the movement per se. For example, the name of the martial art "karate-do" translated literally simply means "the way of the empty hand." From a superficial viewpoint, this means that by using this fighting technique you are able to defend yourself with empty hands—without holding any weapon—against a stronger opponent (also physically stronger). When looking more in depth, this sport also includes the concept of emptiness of the mind for channeling the concentration of force—psychic as well as physical.

If you are throwing your knives for an hour, then that hour belongs to you and your throwing weapons; everything else has to stay outside your mind and has to wait. Don't worry, it will still be there afterward!

In addition, there is a nice concomitant effect in that the thrower is immediately—within a second—rewarded by the sound of hitting for his or her sportive zeal. A good performance of your throwing move immediately leads to its confirmation and the direct reward for your effort. Here I once again take the direct comparison to the center forward of a soccer team who, in the worst case, during the entire game won't get a single usable chance of shooting a goal and at the end of the day won't get a sportive reward.

The Potato Chips Effect

While with many kinds of sports you are indeed happy when the hard training is finally coming to an end, and, in a few minutes, you will be able to take a shower and then go back home, strangely it is exactly the opposite for knife throwing. I call this the potato chips effect. This phenomenon is widespread: you open a bag of wonderful potato chips and are unable to stop eating until the last crumb has been eaten.

Transferred to throwing, it is a fact that even beginners realize during the first couple of training sessions. Sometimes he or she has reached the point at which stopping voluntarily is hardly possible. "Addiction" starts! We simply want more! In many of these cases of "severe addiction," only vanishing daylight in the evening causes us throwers to finally release our weapons from an already hurting hand.

Thus the circle closes, because this is the cause for being fascinated by the sport of throwing: first, it isn't very fatiguing for the body, meaning you can do it over a long period of time without showing any sign of fatigue up to an old age!

Second, throwing promotes concentration and channels your attention onto two essential points and nothing else. Third, it is the perfected art of your coordinative skills, which in case of the successful interaction of mind and muscles immediately results in the acoustic and fourth reward: "thunk."

20 Material Care and Maintenance

Sometimes when I see the totally scratched, chipped, and rusted—almost shabby—weapons of some thrower friends, I have a strong feeling of compassion toward the blades. Although it is logical, on the one hand, that our knives can't be highly polished, high-quality collector's items but pure sport tools, on the other hand, in the same way as bicycle racers polish and maintain their bicycle or sport divers keep their equipment intact, we, too, should not deny a minimum of maintenance to our basic sport equipment.

This doesn't have only purely aesthetic reasons, but moreover concrete and practical ones: our weapons, in training as well as competition, have to endure hard and rough use that, after some time, inevitably leaves traces on the blades. This is especially valid if you have only a single target at your disposal and throw series of three or even six knives at your target. In earlier times we even conducted our contests this way. For practical reasons, this was changed in 2007.

Blade Maintenance

With this kind of training, knife collisions are no rare event. As a result, small but sharp splinters can be split from a knife. Now imagine briefly that you make a knife throw like in the Wild West with such an untended "scraggy knife": you let the knife fly and immediately wonder about the stinging pain in your index finger.

This will probably happen to you only once. After elaborately removing the tiny metal sliver from your finger with tweezers and a safety pin, you will surely treat your knife better and more carefully in the future. I recommend in general to carefully look at your knives each time after they hit the target. Mark even the slightest damage and, if possible, work it out immediately.

You can do so by means of a metal file or abrasive paper, or by using an angular grinder or a drilling machine with a serrated grinder. The latter is indeed the quickest and cleanest means. You can also polish your throwing weapons wonderfully by means of a serrated grinder and make a good impression in competition. It also expresses

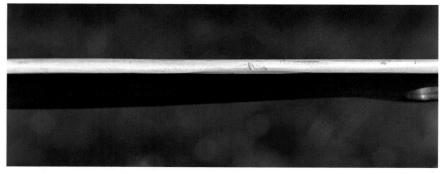

Typical nick on the blade's back caused by collision with another knife at the target. Best you remove this damage as soon as possible.

114

Nicks on the blade edge are also the result of hard contact of metal on metal. Here only grinding helps.

Typical notches on an ax head caused by collision with another ax at the target.

a certain inner attitude toward our sport when we keep our weapons visibly in a good state. Of course, for pragmatic reasons this means we always keep the tips and ends of our knives sharp, because these are the points that hit the wood of the target disks.

115

Conservation

After the season is over, maybe in deepest winter—in case you want to have a break for several weeks—it makes sense to oil your throwing knives. Ideal for this is Klever Ballistol weapon oil; it protects from corrosion, and you will enjoy your edged weapons for a longer time.

For temperatures lower than freezing, it is not recommended to do your training "outdoors," not only because of cold hands but because with freezing temperatures, the water accumulated in the soft wood of the disks freezes and the wooden disks become as hard as concrete. You could as well throw against a stone wall, which is why I personally like to take a break under these circumstances and wait until it gets warmer again.

But don't forget: before you start throwing again, remove the oil residues from your knives as thoroughly as possible because otherwise you will make so-called oil throws, with the knives slipping from your hand and flying off toward the sky in a steep arc.

Thin and slight rust residues can be polished off with abrasive fine-grit paper or with a serrated grinder. Alternatively, you can use a bit of water and a "Zitronenstein" (literally "lemon stone," a substance used for cleaning chrome and tiles in the kitchen). Afterward dry thoroughly, because otherwise the rust will be back in no time.

You should always store your knives in a dry place. This means don't store them outdoors in the tool shed or garden shack, because the air moisture in there is usually too high.

22 The Best Age

Which age is the best to start our sport? "The early bird . . ." is a proverb that fits for ax and knife throwing, as well as for any other kind of sportive action. But since the safe use of our sports equipment is an elementary aspect of our sport, a minimum age should apply. When compared directly with gymnastics, to which a four-year-old child can be led in a playful way, throwing sport has a different approach. On the one hand, a child has to be able to grasp that in our sport— similar to archery—the task is to safely handle a weapon without endangering any participant or bystander. The child also has to have the required strength to be able to throw the weapon.

From my experience, I can tell that ten years old is a good age for starting. This is valid for boys as well as for girls, because at that age my niece Kim started her training under my supervision, and only two years later and totally surprisingly, she became the youngest European champion to date in the women's rating (short-distance knife throwing, 3 meters, Big European Throwers Meeting, Czech Republic, 2008).

It is recommended to keep the weight of the throwing knives within reasonable limits—between 10½ and 14 ounces if possible. Conversely, the weight should also not be too low; otherwise the joints would be stressed too much, as is the case with adults. For beginners, good knife models for children and youngsters are the "Artistenwurfmesser" by Haller, the "Dismissal" by Condor, and the "Perfect Balance Thrower" by Cold Steel.

A throwing ax shouldn't be too heavy either if it is to be thrown by children or youngsters. This means it shouldn't weigh much more than the required minimum of 1 pound, 1 ounce. My first choice would be the "Trail Hawk" by Cold Steel, which weighs about 1⅓ pounds. Its wooden shaft can easily be cut down to the size appropriate for the body of a young thrower.

Now, you have to add the aspect of safety: children and youngsters should be under the supervision of an adult as soon as they start their training. I actually see a direct supervision of children and youngsters between ages ten and sixteen as indispensable. It just doesn't work without this, but you can sell it brilliantly as a "joint training" so the youngsters won't feel patronized. Between ages sixteen and eighteen

Perfect foot position—the author's niece during throwing

it depends on the circumstances: if a reasonable young man of seventeen trains on his own for a little while in a private, fenced garden, from my point of view this is quite acceptable.

A different situation is given if four teenagers are throwing together—maybe two of them are less reasonable, or even careless. In case one of them hits on the great idea to compete in "throwing silhouettes" for a dare, I'd rather be with them the entire time to prevent this before something really bad happens.

But to all parents whose son or daughter has brought home this book: knife and ax throwing really is a sport like any other, and dangers to one's health are lurking in playing soccer or handball, driving a racing bike, or doing artistic gymnastics. During all previous competitions in which I participated in Europe and the US, there has been only a single light injury, and this was the result of one of my thrower friends hitting on the idea during a break to juggle his tomahawks, and while doing so he inadvertently grasped the sharp end.

There is an additional aspect: how to recognize and reasonably deal with dangers of all kinds is also part of growing up for young people. With these they can mature and collect the experiences they need in life as adults. By the way, with respect to this, Americans accomplish the best work with young talents. Here the kids are introduced to and trained in knife throwing quite early.

23 How "Sportsmanlike" Is Knife and Ax Throwing?

Each of you who want to start with sportive knife and ax throwing doesn't have to be a "Tarzan" or "Ironman" to do so. An average strength in your arms is totally sufficient for this in the beginning, and you don't need a medical certificate either. In the end you will surely know best what you are able to do and for how long.

A specialty of our sport is that you can perform it up to an advanced age—and without looking involuntarily comical. Throwing is less about raw physical force or marathon shape and more about technique, experience, precision of movement, fine motor skills, strength of nerves, and constant training. Sometimes even a person in their midseventies is able to demonstrate these qualities impressively. But as soon as you want to intensify your training and even want to familiarize yourself with long-distance throwing (the rules for this are in "Sporting Competitions, Thrower Meetings, Championships, and Rules"), it can't hurt to add a few items to your training.

To keep your shape at this level over a longer period of time, I recommend a short and sweet but also regular additional training, mainly for building up strength of the upper torso and arms. It doesn't need to be longer than fifteen minutes per unit, and about three units per week are sufficient. Ideally you train this combination every forty-eight hours, because your muscles use the time of the break to adapt to the new conditions and react to this by growing. In sport science this is called "overcompensation." This means your muscles try to always be a tad better than the next load of force presumably needs. It is my belief that this rule also holds for the mind, which can be trained in a similar way. You should allow this rest to your body!

As a positive side effect, this power supplemental training prevents the one-sided development of your muscles, which in the long run would lead to suffering of both your body halves. After all, you always throw with one side of your body. This phenomenon is known from some tennis players who have forgotten about their compensation training: on the left, a bloodless drumstick, and on the right, a forearm like Sylvester Stallone's!

A perfect strength training is always set up in such a way that your muscles are trained to the brink of exhaustion. This may happen rather quickly if you train the individual muscles reasonably isolated. Sportive throwing is foremost a sport of the upper part of your body, so you ought to mainly train your back, chest, shoulders, abdominals, and arms. In all there are four exercises—actually only three, because you can train your biceps and triceps in a single exercise.

A simple but stable leather belt is best suited as a training tool for workouts.

127

Your only training tool is yourself, meaning your body weight or your other body half as an antagonist, and you may also use a towel, a trouser belt, and a wristwatch with a seconds hand or stopwatch function. This way your training is absolutely free of charge and you save the fees for the fitness club.

We always do three or four rounds (or "sets") of every individual exercise, with a break of about thirty seconds in between. There is no reason for despair when the number of achievable repetitions slowly goes down during the second and third sets; this is an indication of correct training, because the muscle has to become tired. Don't be afraid of aching muscles, because this is a sign of a successful workout. Growth always starts with aching muscles! "Warming up," by the way, is not necessary, because training itself provides for this.

Workout 1

We start with chest-triceps-back. The classic push-up is still the easiest and best. Important here: the palms of your hands are set at shoulder's width apart and face inward slightly, the back should not sag, and you push from your chest and triceps. The back, as well as the muscles of your core and buttocks, have to perform additional sustaining work— best imagine that you would have to hold a coin with your buttocks— and both muscle sections are also trained in this way passively.

Three or four sets of fifteen repetitions, with a break of thirty seconds each in between, and you will know for a start what you have done. If this doesn't work neatly at the beginning, at first you can perform the mitigated version with your knees resting on a towel. Nobody is watching you, and you don't have to demonstrate anything. The point is only clean, effective execution. Conversely, you will get to the point sometime that with normal push-ups you will hardly break a sweat. When you are able to do fifty repetitions in one go, then try deep, slow push-ups between two chairs. Your chest will burn like fire; this is an absolute growth turbo!

Workout 1: Push-ups are still the best method for strengthening the chest muscles. You can see how the hands are set on the ground, facing inward about a shoulder's width apart.

Workout 2

With isokinetic upper-arm training we train the biceps and triceps at the same time. The triceps now receive some work to do for the second time. This is good the way it is, because the triceps also have to do the main work during throwing; an additional reason to care for it in an especially considerate way. The biceps, in contrast, have the important task of stopping the throwing movement and thus preventing us from hitting the elbow joint with the circular move of the arm.

Take your trouser belt in hand and create a tension between your arms with about 70 percent of your maximum force as you can see (you will have to try to feel it). Then pull both arms as a "power unit" slowly downward ten times while keeping the tension all the time.

While doing so, breathe calmly and steadily. If possible, try to keep this exercise up for thirty seconds, then have a break of thirty seconds.

This movement will be easier for you if you do it with an implied rider's stance. This way your legs will also have to do a bit. Change body sides after repeating three sets. In all, the exercises will take about six minutes, not more!

Workout 2: This exercise is for training your biceps and triceps. The arms are moved upward and downward with a tension of about 70 percent of your strength for about thirty seconds.

Workout 3

Isokinetic back and shoulder training: take your belt again and now push it with permanent tension outward, again with about 70 percent of your maximum force. Now you slowly guide this "power unit" upward from the level of your waistband to high above your head while keeping the tension. This, too, is done according to the well-proven recipe of thirty seconds of work followed by a break of the same length. Finished after three minutes!

Workout 3: With isokinetic back and shoulder training, the belt is lifted from the level of your hips to over your head and back again, using about 70 percent of the maximum tensile strength of your arms.

Workout 4

This isokinetic chest training is something for really hard-boiled people, but you can also put it in first position and use it for warming up your chest: we again take the belt, and this time grip it crossed over. Then once again perform a "power unit" pushing inward with permanent

Workout 4: The isokinetic training for your chest muscles is similar to the exercise from workout 2, but here you hold the belt differently.

tension and, similar to the back exercise in workout 3, slowly guide it upward and downward between waistband and face level.

Even if you perform all four exercises in a row without any dawdling worth mentioning, you have just trained for a quarter of an hour. Isokinetic training has two big advantages: first, it saves time and is efficient. Second, it is highly effective with respect to muscle growth, because in contrast to training with free weights, with this form of training the resistance is constantly at the same level, regardless of which angle your muscle is working at in a given moment. In contrast, a dumbbell or other type of free weight has only a rather small degree of efficiency.

Please remember that buildup and training of your muscles are not restricted to the location of a fitness club or gym, because your muscles really don't care about where they receive their training. The only important thing is a sufficient training resistance of reasonable intensity and duration and afterward a sufficient break for regeneration, because everything needs its time. But here I explicitly promise you enormous growth of power when you do this training three times a week. Just wait for half a year or a complete year and you will be enormously impressed! And be happy!

And if somebody asks you a few months from now whether you have started to visit a fitness club because you "somehow look better," then think of my words and grin to yourself contentedly. You have earned it, and I won't tell anybody!

With an Isokinator you can measure the force used during the four workout exercises. For this you hold the device in exactly the same way you hold the leather belt.

Sporting Competitions, Thrower Meetings, Championships, and Rules

The Basic Conditions

Eventually, you will have dealt with the throwing sport for about a year. You have found the throwing item perfectly made for you, and you have trained with lots of fun, joy, and dedication. You now feel quite sure when dealing with your missiles and have built up and prepared yourself well. One morning you may wake with the thought that it is about time to compete with other throwers in a friendly and sportive contest to experience in direct comparison where you stand.

At the moment it is still very easy to directly sign up and register for an important, great international contest (European and World Championships). On the website www.knifethrowing.info, under "thrower meetings," you can always find current announcements for upcoming competitions together with an online form for signing up. The fees for participating are within manageable limits and at the moment are usually between $55 and $90.

Traveling to places of competition is up to the individual. I personally drive to most contests in my own car. On the way there, I often collect friends at their homes or from the nearest airport, then camp locally, as close as possible or even at the site of the competition. Many befriended throwers often share a hotel room in the vicinity or create "tent castles" at camping areas, at which there may still be a lot of activity going on in the evenings after the competition and until late at night. All this happens according to previous agreements and is purely a private matter, because in our sport there are no generous sponsors or large societies that would take over the costs for our trips.

Worldwide (as of May 2017) there are always about 140 to 170 throwers attending our big international contests and, since 2014, our officially announced World Championships of Knife Throwers. As mentioned previously, attending is still possible for everybody, but we rigorously sort out the competitors in our qualifying contests. In the end, only the best 20 percent of all participating throwers qualify for the final contest, which consists of a demanding throwing marathon of a total of sixty throws from various distances.

This hard slog is done separately for axes and knives and requires a lot of power, previous training effort, experience, and skill. Since 2008 a different rating for women has been initiated because their number has grown steadily over time.

The Competitive Situation

To prepare yourself better strategically for upcoming big international contests, I recommend attending smaller, national friendship competitions beforehand and also participating in international contests and meetings that take place nationwide every now and then. There you can breathe a bit of competitive air and may also get to know some of the masters of our sport.

One thing you will immediately realize during the action is that there is a huge difference between flawlessly throwing a series of "bull's eyes" alone in your own garden and having countless eyes follow you during a competition. Not to forget the referee with a clipboard and the score sheet in hand, standing next to you, who eyeballs you critically and then asks, "Ready?" Now it counts. Right here and now, when you want to throw your very first competition series of twenty-one throws, and it dawns on you that there are possibly a lot of viewers staring at you.

Sport throwing in a competitive situation can well be compared with a penalty shoot-out in a decisive soccer match: of course, the professional soccer player has trained and internalized the penalty kick thousands of times and in different variations during practice. He or she already controls it in almost a deep sleep, but under (felt) pressure and with the factor of stress, misses are not uncommon in such decisive situations of the game. Even with absolute top professionals!

The competitive situation is always decisive for the performance.

Coping with Stress

With respect to the topic "Choking under Pressure"—the sportive "dropout" under conditions of stress, implying mental weakness—here are a few brief tips on my part that may help you if needed, as well as with other kinds of sport or comparable situations in life or examinations. These have proven to be successful—at least they have worked for me consistently.

Important for the first time: you will automatically sense a quickened heartbeat, sometimes even up to your neck. Try to relax by inhaling deeply and exhaling consciously three times prior to your first throw. Bring back to your mind that you are a newbie in this sport; you are not watched as closely as the perennial favorites. Start relaxed; this is just an issue of making a good impression. The score is not settled before it's over, and especially in our sport the final results are often a big surprise.

Total focus during competition

You should also remind yourself time and again that you are here because throwing is a lot of fun for you—regardless of whether you are at home or at this place. After throwing the first series of three, you will become more relaxed and also better.

Take a little breathing break prior to the final throw of each of your series of three, because, on the basis of personal experience, this final attempt often results in a miss since you start to mentally "let go" and your concentration diminishes a bit.

At the beginning of your competition career, it may also be helpful to leave your "fan club"—your spouse, partner, parents, or significant others—at home, because you create additional internal stress when you have the feeling that you have to "deliver" especially good results. You are also better able to focus on yourself. But this is up to you, because some sportsmen are fired up to top performance only when knowing that their fair maiden is watching.

Disciplines and Rules

Our main disciplines of sportive knife and ax throwing are precision-throwing contests from different throwing distances. Meanwhile, these precision-throwing contests are also the qualifying disciplines for participating in the finals of the big international competitions. By means of a sophisticated average coefficient resulting from the total points achieved in all thrown distances (with throws from a longer distance having a higher value than those thrown from a short distance), only the best 20 percent of throwers are allowed to participate in the finals. Thus it is ensured that only the best and most consistent top sports people are fighting for the crown, because a "lucky punch" in just one discipline is only of limited value now. This makes the finals all the more attractive for spectators, because they exclusively get to see designated high quality during the final competitions.

Besides these main disciplines, there are also exciting duels during which two lottery-selected throwers have to compete on a knockout basis. Whoever draws the knife quickest from the holster and hits the given field of the target from a minimum distance of 10 feet first moves on one round, while the loser drops out. From my experience, duel throwing is very popular with spectators but usually takes up a lot of time because of the high number of competitors.

The hits are even determined electronically with a measuring device developed just for this purpose, to an exactness of one-hundredth

During the contest it sometimes makes sense to insert a short training unit; here, throwing from a distance of 23 feet.

of a second. My thrower friend and professional inventor Walter Steinbeck from Regensburg, Germany, invented and constructed this device. This was indeed urgently needed, because top duel throwers draw their knives, aim, throw, and often also hit within a time span of just 0.8 seconds. If two such top sports people duel, the eyes of the referee are soon overstrained.

For the friends of instinctive throwing, there has been a possibility for competing since 2014. No-spin as well as half-spin throwers are sent on a demanding route requiring throws starting with a distance of 10 feet and stepwise up to 23 feet. This is no job for beginners but is exclusively reserved for well-trained specialists. I also want to mention that this discipline so far is not run regularly during every world championship of knife throwers; the particular event organizer at the site decides on it. For example, during the 2015 world championship in Great Britain, this special competition was not held.

Instinctive throwing is especially popular with Russian, Polish, and Czech throwers. These are the countries where most no-spin and half-spin throwers pursue their passion. Meanwhile, it has its due niche even in American competition and is a regular part of the contests.

Last but not least, distance throwing is also an elementary discipline in contests and is very attractive for spectators. Here, the thrower has the task of getting a valid score with three throws onto the large hitting area of the target disk. If he or she succeeds, they can move back in the distance field, repeat the attempt, and so on. In the end, the thrown distances with knives are just a tad below 65 feet and even farther away with the throwing ax. At the time this book was finalized, the world record was 89½ feet thrown by Czech Stanyslav Havel, and it can be admired in a YouTube video.

Rules for Knife and Ax Throwing

Only those knives with a length of 9 inches and up are permitted. Special constructions with multiple tips at the handle or guard for "always sticking" are prohibited. A throwing knife is allowed to have only one tip, and, after being thrown, it has to stick in the disk with just this tip. Aerodynamic throwing weapons ("dart" knives) or aerodynamic add-ons (such as feathers, bands, or threads) are naturally out of the question. At the same time, the width of the blade is not allowed to exceed 2⅓ inches at its broadest spot. With axes, the maximum width can be 4¾ inches.

The highest cut ring counts as a valuation hit. In case a decision is debated, the referee always has the final say. By the way, he or she is always right, regardless of the issue. This means don't bother starting a discussion. If there really is justified doubt with respect to the valuation of a hit, you have the right to involve the main valuation referee, but his or her decision afterward is the ultimate, ironclad law.

The main discipline consists of a series with twenty-one throws per distance (with the knife, these are 3, 5, and 7 meters; with the ax, 4, 5, and 7 meters). The throws are made with three knives or axes toward three targets set up next to each other. These targets are constructed in such a way that the center bull's eye is at a height of between 51 and 63 inches above the ground. With good old mathematics, this means that you now face seven rounds with three throws each. After many years of testing, this has proven to be the most practical way of sportive throwing.

No more than ten years ago, there were exclusively single throws toward only one target; the throwers were standing (too) close to each other, and, for safety reasons, the throws had to be executed simultaneously

141

on command of the referee ("Get ready for throwing!"—"Throw!"—"Pick up!"). Due to the greatly increased number of participants, individual throws take too much time. It has been proven that a series of three is thrown faster, and the throwers don't have to bother about what happens in the neighboring lane 26 feet away, meaning they can focus on themselves. Throwing at three targets also has the simple, practical justification that collisions between thrown weapons can be avoided. This was not always the case and, in earlier times, quite often led to frustrations when the thrower managed a great hit on the bull's eye but one of his knives or axes was already sticking there, thus causing a collision.

By the way, it is obligatory since 2016 to throw three knives or axes of the same model. Thus you should immediately equip yourself with at least a set of three of the same model for training at home, too, because this way you will be better "in the flow" in the course of the competition and you will also be finished sooner.

I don't believe it is reasonable to use different knives or axes for different distances (e.g., a special knife for the short distance, another model for the distance of 7 meters), because in the end, when you have qualified for the finals, you have to make do with a single model for all distances. Changing the knife or ax type during the contest is not permitted, with only a few exceptions; for example, if an ax handle breaks.

Back to the target: the target in sportive competition consists of ringed disks made of soft wood. The bull's eye has a diameter of 4 inches. This sounds large, but from your training experience you surely know quite well now how small this black dot looks from the required distance to the target.

A hit in the bull's eye will give you five points. The next lower rings each have a width of 2 inches, resulting in the target area on the disk having a diameter of exactly 20 inches. The values are one point less

A target disk with different-colored rings for evaluating the throws. In this case, thirteen points have been achieved: two times bull's eye (*yellow*) with five points each and once three points (*blue*).

for each; thus four points, three points, two points, and one point. The highest cut ring is counted as a hit, even if it is only scratched slightly. On the basis of experience, the valuation is always made in favor of the thrower in case of doubt and with marginal hits.

Using arithmetic, with your twenty-one throws you can theoretically achieve a highest score of 105 points when always hitting the bull's eye. I can intimate that, especially for the short distance with the knife, we are not very far away from this: 102 points has been thrown from a distance of 10 feet using a knife. Stanyslav Havel from the Czech Republic in 2016 managed 105 points with an ax from 13 feet.

Also important: the distance marker on the ground must not be overstepped (similar to broad jumps). According to the latest update of the rules and with strict interpretation, the contestant is not even allowed to touch the mark with the tip of the shoes! This can be decisive if you belong to the stretching "swingers" who like to bend their upper torso forward quite a bit, maybe even while lifting their rear leg.

Here you must be very careful, because as soon as you step up to the mark or even tiptoe a bit across it, the referee has the right to value the throw at zero points, even though your knife sticks really neatly right in the center of the bull's eye.

But in turn you are allowed to step back as far as 6½ feet behind the target line in case this is required by your throwing technique. Although this is disadvantageous, because you are giving away precious distance (or rather nearness), it is not against the rules.

Don't bother with discussions after overstepping, because they are of no avail. If you are a nuisance to the referee about this, he or she even has the right to send you off. During the ten years of my career, I have not experienced this in competition.

When you have finished your series, don't immediately run forward in a hurry to check your hits, because the referee with a nitpicking interpretation may see this as overstepping during the final throw. Shot putters and hammer throwers even have to leave the throwing ring to

During a contest, always keep an eye on the distance bar. As in other sports, overstepping results in an invalid throw.

SPORTING COMPETITIONS, THROWER MEETINGS, CHAMPIONSHIPS, AND RULES

the back as soon as they are finished. To leave it at the front raises the red flag: invalid. Thus, rather briefly stay at the spot—this also conveys a confident impression—then walk toward the disks together with the referee when he values your hits and writes them down.

Before it gets serious in the contest, you always have the option of throwing a trial series of three throws beforehand. I have been in the business for a long time and am an old hand, but I don't want to abstain from this trial run and always like to do this. It relaxes you, gets you acquainted with the competition lane, and gives you a good feeling. And if a knife falls down during this trial run, you can cheer yourself up, because this is not decisive. You just made the "bad one"; now only "good ones" follow. And in case all goes well from the beginning, then you are on the right track anyway.

Last but not least: loud cursing after a miss is internationally seen as gross and has to be avoided under all circumstances. In the Anglo-American realm the four-letter word starting with "f" is a special sacrilege that can cause shocked embarrassment for spectators as well as the referee, so please repress it. Although thoughts are free, they ought to be unheard!

The Grand Finale

In the event that you made it and find yourself among the best 20 percent of all the participants, I say "congratulations," because now you are among the best of the best. Your consistent training has paid off. And for you this means the final contest!

This contest, in turn, is a precision competition, now in the form of a so-called walk-back. This expression means that after the first series of three throws from a distance of 3 meters (4 meters with the axe), you walk backward for at least 1 meter and throw another series of three until you have reached the 7-meter mark (10 meters with the axe!). Unlike in American contests, here the number of rotations needed by your knife doesn't matter, so in theory you can throw all distances with "no spin."

With this contest you also have the chance to throw the full distance on a trial basis. This is a good opportunity for warming up prior to the valued contest throws, and thus a chance you always ought to take. You

Warming up prior to the round during the 2010 world cup in Austin, Texas. During US competitions there are no qualification rounds.

throw a set of three each from the distances of 3, 4, 5, 6, and 7 meters (4, 5, 7, 8, and 10 meters with the axe) and have to do this four times. In all there are sixty throws, so you can achieve a maximum of 300 points.

The world record with the knife at this time is 274 points, held by American Richard Wesson. The record with the ax was set by my German teammate Werner Lengmüller from Regensburg, with a formidable 264 points. My own best result in competitions with the knife at the moment is 249 points.

This marathon program is a class of its own, and under no circumstances does it work without sufficient training and long-term, optimum preparation. On the one hand you need sufficient power reserves to manage the full distance without lacking fine motor skills and precise aiming. On the other hand, you already should have trained on the designated distances during your time of preparation and thus should not suddenly be surprised by the requirements.

This can easily happen when you are actually not counting on participating in the finals. But let me tell you, sometimes just being in good shape on that day and having a relaxed mind is all that is needed to be among the best. And there is one irrevocable fact in the sport of throwing as well as all other kinds of sport: luck is helpful sometimes, and good training always helps!

Always train the "tricky" distances of 4 and 6 meters at your throwing stand (5 and 8 meters with the axe). Basically you can proceed logically and linearly when counting your distances, with half a rotation occurring per meter (1.5 meters with the axe). Depending on your own throwing style, there may be deviations of about 20 inches, but you already knew that. Maybe you need only two turns with your knife from a distance of 6 meters, but this time experimenting is also part of your preparatory training. It has to be used.

Other Disciplines and Sideshows

The above-described disciplines are our main ones. In addition, the organizers at the competition site often think of further entertainment and exciting "sideshows" to make the contests more fun for all participants—throwers as well as spectators.

Among other things, "speed throwing" has become an established standard. Here, the thrower receives a whole batch of identical throwing knives at his or her disposal and at the same time the task to achieve as many valid hits on the target wood as possible from a distance of at least 3 meters and within twenty seconds. The current record is held by Russian Sergey Fedosenko and consists of an impressive twenty-eight knives!

Meanwhile, the "classic" is not missing either: throwing silhouettes. It is mainly done with knives, and sometimes also with axes. Of course here the targets are not living humans; a life-size image—or photo— is used as a target. This may also be an image of Princess Leia from *Star Wars*, a silhouette of Queen Cleopatra, or something similar.

But the rules are strict: there are 4-inch points arranged around the silhouette image—in all, fifteen—that have to be hit in the correct order, starting in the lower left and continuing around the silhouette from a distance of at least 3 meters. Each hit is awarded five points, but you have to be cautious: if the target figure is as much as scratched, this immediately leads to points being removed! This discipline is a lot of fun for us throwers and is performed tongue-in-cheek. In the course of the competition, this is rather a bit of relaxation and loosening up and is basically not taken as seriously as our main disciplines.

The Mountainman Contest

Contests in sportive knife throwing existed two centuries ago. Hunters, scouts, and trappers were roaming the American forests. All of them had knives, and some also carried a small ax at their belt. If you have a knife at hand in the wilderness, you can use it to make most of the tools or rudimentary weapons needed, and can also use it for constructing some place for dwelling, making firewood, tailoring a leather shirt, and preparing your dinner.

The trappers of the forest area had trained their skills in knife and ax throwing back then and created a sportive competition not needing lots of utensils. They didn't have black, red, and white dyes for a ringed disk, but most westerners had playing cards. Thus it was quickly decided to perform a special precision contest trying to spear the aforementioned playing cards as exactly as possible by means of aimed knife and ax throws.

Today, the "Mountainman Contest" is still held in this archaic form of sportive throwing. It is attractive because of a few specialties: it is quite obvious that this is a Wild West contest because of the contestants' outfits; you will not see anybody attending in their jogging clothes or shorts. Historical western outfits or traditional regional customs are welcome. During the preparatory training throws, you already feel like a time traveler to the past.

There are no official distance markers on the ground either, because the throws are measured with respect to the necessary rotations of the thrown weapon. In the first round of the knife disciplines, throws with a single rotation are usually required; throws of the second round require two rotations. There were no "no-spinners" in the Wild West, and so in the Mountainman contests there are only "spins."

It is up to you to determine at what point in front of the target is where you need exactly a single rotation of your knife or ax, but this doesn't make things easier for you since you are not allowed to use a measuring tape.

By the way, I don't recommend the well-known measure of "counting steps" in case you don't have a measuring device at hand, because the length of your steps may vary without you being aware of it. Counting the number of foot lengths is the most reliable means. For example, I can measure exactly 10.5 lengths with my (European) size 43 boots, and then I stand almost exactly to the inch at a distance of 3 meters in front of the target. A distance of fourteen foot lengths corresponds to 4 meters, and another seven foot lengths add an additional 2 meters to the distance. And since foot lengths put directly one after another don't contain any sources of error worth mentioning, this way of measuring the distance is the safest one.

Another little specialty of this kind of competition: you can leave your throwing knives in the saddlebag, cowboy, because they are no longer permitted. The same is true for axes made completely of steel: the classic Mountainman contest is held exclusively with utility knives and tomahawks with a wooden handle. Each participant has his or her throwing weapon especially tailored to them and with a mandatory visible edge, but this doesn't have to be ground to "hair-cutting sharpness" and can have a handle of wood, horn, leather, or even plastics (e.g., Micarta). Flat handle wraps of paracord or tape are off limits, as are handles of bare steel.

Now the playing cards for hitting are fixed to the round target by means of matches or toothpick halves. The target disk is divided into four quadrants with one playing card each. The final card is placed in the center. If you want to train this discipline at home, please don't use any nails for pinning the cards; it is almost a natural law that the blade tip will hit the nail heads. What this means for your knives, you can imagine.

Now the competitor has the task to hit the pinned cards in exactly the required order, starting with the card in the upper left quadrant and then continuing clockwise: upper right, lower right, lower left, and finally the card in the center. Then the resulting points are added: if you hit a card in the center so well that its border isn't cut, such a "center cut" will give you three points. If you hit the card only at the margins or touch it only slightly, this simple "cut" will give you two points. Here the slightest deformations of the card will be counted in your favor, in case you just "pushed" the card a little bit. If you hit only the quadrant and not the card itself, you will be credited with one point anyway.

One thing is clear in any case: misses always result in zero points even when you hit the card (e.g., with the handle). The knife or ax has to stick in the target in a valid way. And you will also receive a "zero" if you hit the card but it's the wrong one. The correct order has to be

During the "Mountainman Contest" you throw at playing cards that have to be hit in a predetermined order. At left is a simple "cut"; at right, a "center cut."

151

strictly maintained, even if it is just to exclude random success or the famous "lucky punch" of a lucky guy or gal. As a maximum you can achieve fifteen points in one round of throwing.

These competition guidelines represent just a coarse framework. Individual disciplines are often varied and modified a bit, depending on the event. Sometimes there are contests requiring knife throws with three rotations; sometimes you may have to start your series of throws with a different card. On rare occasions you may alternately have to throw your ax immediately after throwing your knife, which is very demanding. But you always have to throw with the required western knife and the tomahawk toward the playing cards in the predetermined order.

For obvious reasons, we throwers have great fun with this discipline, because in this way we can feel like a westerner or scout in the Rocky Mountains of the nineteenth century.

25 Throwing:
Always a Matter of Nerves

This conclusion regularly proves to be true. As with all kinds of sport, for us, too, sportive preparation and throwing techniques are the main aspect of training in our special precision sport. Most competitors who sign up for our contests are usually well trained and are quite good at throwing. But often the wheat is separated from the chaff not in accordance with the better throwing skills of individual athletes, but mainly due to their strength of nerve and experience.

I can reveal to you that I, too, had to do some catching-up work in this area. But you now have the great advantage that I know both sides very well and can save you a lot of caloric effort and frustration by taking you with me "on the trip" right now.

Interestingly, I was hardly nervous at all during my very first contests between 2005 and 2008, but in hindsight I am able to explain this. I was a newbie on the scene, which back then was rather limited, felt more or less unobserved, and, in principle, didn't have much to lose. At the beginning I thought that there were indeed better participants attending than me, and I would hardly have any chance of winning, or even of stepping onto the rostrum. My only goal was to make a good impression and not to hold the "red lantern" in the end.

This worked out quite well, but in 2007 and 2008 I was suddenly and surprisingly able to win four times in major European throwing contests, and then it hit: an appearance on the *Galileo* show of the TV

Foto: istockphoto.com/Spanic

Meditation exercises may help enhance your ability to focus. This is especially important during competitions.

channel "ProSieben" under the title "Europe's Best Knife Thrower"—even while the contest was still ongoing—and immediately afterward there was a request for a live performance on a Saturday evening western show of the TV channel "Sat 1." Things were happening at a breakneck pace.

The latter project was a rather gruesome experience because I was totally inexperienced in this métier and now, after the announcement of the show master, was standing live in a crowded TV studio in front of 400 people. Good that my pulse wasn't transmitted live as well! My short performance was quite okay, although the material I had at my disposal—the throwing wall—was far from what I had desired.

But the previous dress rehearsal had been absolutely catastrophic, and during its course I really wished the ground would swallow me up. In the first round I had the task to throw six throwing knives from a distance of 7 meters onto playing cards and a western-type "wanted" poster of the show master. The idea of the target design had come from me, because I wanted to display sportive-oriented throwing instead of the well-known (and banal) vaudeville act of silhouette throwing.

The wooden throwing wall was centered on a rollaway platform to be able to quickly roll it in and out of the studio and also to be able to turn it around. This had worked perfectly the first time the previous day, despite Murphy's law and the prominent show master. But now the nice props people, during the dress rehearsal, made the decisive mistake when measuring the distance not to put the end of the measuring tape at the target, but at the platform's base—and thus almost an entire 3¼ feet in front of the target. Already when I was swinging backward and aiming at the target from my position for the first time, I had the strange feeling that something was wrong, but in a studio the perception of measurements and dimensions can play tricks on you.

You can imagine the results: I made a 7-meter throw on a target exactly 8 meters away, and, of course, this couldn't end well. Thus I had four misses in a row with the knives after three and a half rotations, hitting the target with a loud bang and handle first. And this happened in front of the entire crew and the eyes of the notables who were present! It didn't help much that my innocence was proven in the end, after detecting the measuring error, because I just wanted "to get out of here!"

A thousand things went through my head at that time: "Everybody is thinking that guy can't do it at all!" "I hope there are not many people watching this live later!" "Can't they just cut out this story in the end?" "I will also abstain from my pay." "Wouldn't it have been better if at least my wife had stayed at home?" "Gee, that's going to be fun!" I could continue this enumeration for quite a while.

I had an awfully queasy feeling prior to my appearance, and it is just nonsense that a bad dress rehearsal is always an omen for a good show. A bad rehearsal just lets you appear in a bad mood and with belly cramps—this is the cruel and naked truth! Luckily I fought quite bravely in the live show, and, apart from a small wobble with the tomahawk, everything went quite fine for me. But this experience was a formative one for me.

From today's point of view, out of inexperience I had naturally made a few unnecessary but decisive mistakes that I would not repeat again and haven't repeated again since that time:

- The most important point: You never start with the most difficult discipline in a live performance (e.g., the 7-meter distance with the knife). A high jumper doesn't put the bar up to his or her personal record performance, but slowly works up to top level. All of this follows the rule "from easy to difficult," and the spectator doesn't even have to recognize this. In the end, on the stage even the short distance of 4 meters looks quite far away for the audience.

- Do it yourself! Decisive technical preparations should not be left to laypersons! I personally should have measured the distance and checked it again immediately beforehand. I also should have helped construct and set up the throwing wall. But I don't want to leave out the fact that the supportive attendants provided by the TV channel at the site were always nice, polite, and exceptionally friendly to make me feel very welcome as a participant of the show. This I want to explicitly say.

- The program is determined by me! Nobody else knows better which kinds of show elements can be created from sportive throwing, and how you can line them up in a reasonable way to make them attractive for a public audience.

This short performance in late fall 2008 had a very long-lasting effect and also had consequences: in the following competitions, my memory reliably and totally unconsciously reminded me of the failed dress rehearsal and the unpleasant and bad squeezing in my lower abdomen. Between 2009 and 2011 in competition, I distinctly stayed behind my usually available proficiency level. The worst anger, of course, is the anger about oneself, and this actually doesn't make things easier.

At times I had the feeling I would lose the joy I had with my sport. And when, for example, I was able to regularly achieve ninety points and more in training from a distance of 5 meters but during competitions got fewer than seventy, then I recognized that the cause could not be lack of technical skills but rather was related to my nerves.

I discovered the technical expression "choking under pressure," which is quite often used in top competitive sports. It actually means "suffocating from the pressure"—a decline in performance caused by nervous stress and expecting too much of oneself.

This phenomenon exists in almost all kinds of sport where competition conditions and (assumed!) pressure rule: the top center forward misses the goal by miles when shooting the penalty kick that she was so certain to score; the world-class sprinter goofs his third start attempt and is disqualified; the diver rotates too far, loses orientation, and lands in the water back first; and the boxer is distracted, thus drops his cover, and receives a knockout blow. And the sport thrower feels this slight trembling of the hand, one's own heartbeat, and asks himself or herself what this strange thing may be they are holding in their hand right now. In such a mental state, the result of throwing quickly becomes a matter of pure luck. So I knew there was really hard work ahead for me. The solution was mental training.

Back at home sweet home, the elementary question arose: "Why do you do this sport at all?" The answer to this followed quickly and in a kind of inner dialogue: "Because I can do it and because I have fun doing it!" Query by my subconsciousness: "And why don't you simply have fun during competition and relax? In the same way as you do in the garden at home?" My answer (already slightly annoyed): "Stupid question, because it is about something!" Next query and statement: "Oh, really? What's so great about it? Maybe you win next time; maybe you will be third. At some other time you may be the fourth or fifth! So what? You can't always be at the top of the rostrum, so just let go and stay calm." Now my head again, slightly ill tempered: "It is easy for you to talk like this; you don't have to stand there in the front line and have to throw!"

The best tip came in the end: "Does it matter? To whom do you still have to prove anything? Everybody knows you can throw well, so just have a lot of fun out in this great landscape and enjoy all these great vibes! You are among good friends here!" This hit home!

After I had internalized these few but important points, things went upward again in 2012, since I was now totally laid back and noticeably less ambitiously uptight. I have learned to forgive my mistakes and in such a case tell myself that maybe I'll be better in the next round or the next discipline, or maybe as late as next year.

A big international contest offers you so many chances that one "blown" series in a single discipline doesn't count that much. Meanwhile, it even happens that I feel almost as relaxed in the contests as during training in my garden at home, that I enjoy throwing in front of a big audience and "delivering," and that in some disciplines I am able to start with complete inner calmness and balance.

As a conclusion, you ought to internalize the following tenets and repeat them in your head a few times like mantras:

- You can throw and you have lots of fun doing it, regardless of where you are! So just laugh for a change!

- As a newbie in contests, there is no reason for being excited. You are not under surveillance because you are new here. Thus relax and just make a good impression. The score is not settled before it's over anyway!

- For "old hands," you have already delivered a few highlights in the past; you don't have to prove to anyone that you can throw. Just have a lot of fun and enjoy it! You are among good friends here, and the stage is set for you alone. In the end, as soon as a year from now, nobody will remember who achieved which placement and when.

- A miss is not the end of the world and happens even to the best of the best. Breathe deeply once, then stay calm and just continue! There are still a lot of rounds ahead, and your moment surely will come. You feel your heartbeat? Great, because you are actually alive and this makes you awake and attentive.

- Now breathe in and exhale deeply three times, then breathe in only halfway after the last exhale, and now just start throwing like at home—5 meters; there are still only 5 meters here!

- Now focus only on the target and, best, at the "center of the center"—this means a little dot within the "black." Focused in this way, the probability is higher to hit the 4-inch center of the disk.

Examples of a mental "no go" are sayings such as these:

- Pull yourself together!

- Now it counts!

- Now you have to show what you trained for an entire year for!

- Second place is the first loser!

It's best to write these and similarly awful means of pressure, as well as discouraging sayings, on a sheet of paper, scrunch it up, then burn it in your fireplace, because that is the right place for such senseless imperatives. They don't help anybody in any way.

Other good and suitable means for reducing adverse inner stress, on the basis of experience, are small, local contests and thrower meetings in a rather familiar circle before attending larger contests at a later point. You can also ask your training partner at home to film you every once in a while. With this you kill three birds with one stone: first, you create some artificial excitement to which you gradually and playfully get accustomed; second, you have a nice permanent memory of a good training day; and third, you have an excellent tool for error analysis.

To even top the issue off, you can ask the same training partner to write down your results on a sheet of paper on a clipboard the same way a referee does. I can assure you that this feels almost like being in competition and will later, in actual competition, give you inner balance and calmness, as well as routine.

I would be happy if I could spare you some detours in this way that I unnecessarily took. There are no special differences compared to other kinds of sports with a focus on precision and technique.

In addition, mental training and the internalization of elementary tenets work best in a relaxed atmosphere. Try it in the bathtub, during a sauna, or, as an alternative, in the evening with a glass of wine in front of the flickering fireplace, or maybe prior to falling asleep. Envision the contest situation and focus on how you are now finally able to throw while being completely calm, relaxed, and in a state of joyous expectation. How the spectators applaud after a "full house" series (three bull's eyes in a row) and the referee states a brief "nice throwing."

But don't expect any wonders within a short period of time. The human mind can be trained like a muscle, but you can't expect that after training with weights for two weeks you will already look like Wladimir Klitschko. Everything needs its time, but it's surely always good to know that it is worth the effort.

26 Knife Throwing in the Media

In a quiet hour, when I'm thinking about how the art of knife throwing has been presented in the media in the past and present, I come to the conclusion that it needs some kind of "development aid" from our side. On the other hand, our sport, with its exciting contests and the nice people, would hardly have grown into what it is now if earlier performances in shows or adventure movies hadn't left such a strong impression with these people. I don't exclude myself from this.

In TV the old cliché of silhouette throwing quite often still dominates the topic of knife throwing. But other factors are unpredictable here, because the media are not familiar with the throwing scene. Here is a typical presentation created during the shooting of *Kopfball* for the WDR in Cologne, Germany.

As a child, I was less impressed by circus artists but all the more by the precise knife throws of trappers, cowboys, and Native Americans in Wild West movies, who always seemed to be able to knock out their opponents with well-aimed knife throws from almost any distance or were able to hit playing cards in contests. And then there was legendary Tarzan, created by American author Edgar Rice Burroughs, who was able to take down greedy, bloodthirsty poachers with an unerring knife from cover in the deepest African jungle. So knife throwing was always shown either as a martial art or, alternatively, as an amusing entertainment combined with a bit of excitement.

Current Hollywood productions still use the appeal of knife throwing. As examples I would like to mention the movies *The Expendables*, *Gangs of New York*, *Gladiator* (there, it even was a sword), *The Hunted*, *Dance Me Outside*, and the Rambo series. And whenever a knife has to be thrown on German TV, the producers like to get my advice, even if it's just to show the actors a believable and authentic throwing move so that the finished product will look good and realistic. The throw itself is done by me unseen in the background. In the end the viewer will have the impression that the film character just threw his knife in a cool and relaxed way directly past the chief inspector's head and into the trailer's wooden wall.

When I am asked about sportive knife throwing by members of various kinds of media, I often realize that the image of the scantily clad assistant on a turning disk is still present in the minds of my contemporaries. An example of this was the request of a TV production company to participate in a new science program for kids and youngsters that was supposed to clarify knife throwing and look at it scientifically. Of course I received the corresponding script in advance, because in TV nothing is left to chance. One of the questions in there was once again: "When did you throw at a human for the first time?"

The female author for the program was indeed very surprised when I told her on the phone that it is not usual for sport throwers in Europe to do so. Of course I am quite proficient in silhouette throwing, which is not our most difficult exercise anyway because of the rather short distances involved (at least 10 feet in competitions). But we sport throwers perform this discipline only under purely sportive aspects that totally exclude involving a living human in front of the disk and instead let us resort to the images of historic figures or actors. For us, this is foremost an almost demonstrative and philosophical aspect of our sport, which should illustrate and show our peacefulness, nonviolence, and, not least, our sportiveness.

This sportive point of view was first put into perspective by the Westdeutscher Rundfunk (WDR) in the youth program *Kopfball* in 2012. The program wanted to show exactly how to learn and train the art of throwing knives, and what matters when doing so. It should also be clearly explained that the simple and often-repeated silhouette throwing is nothing but a minor "sideshow" of knife throwing, which in our sport has only a subsidiary role.

The authors implemented this last part of the broadcast cleverly. In the first shot it actually looks as if I wanted to throw my knives around the host. To confirm this "false track," I had blindfolded him before. Only after revealing the facts in the second shot did it become obvious that I had thrown my knives only around a mannequin.

I was very happy with the final result. Up to that time our sport had never been better explained and shown on TV, and the high-speed recordings were able to distinctly show many aspects of the motion sequence.

The "development aid" for properly showing and viewing our sport in public thus has just started but is already making good progress. We can't expect any miracles with a throwing-sport history in Europe of just around fifteen years, but we have already achieved quite a lot.

Until recently there has been no professional literature worth mentioning on sportive knife throwing. Dieter Führer from Schongau, Germany, in 2010 wrote the first recommendable book, *Handbuch Messer- und Axtwerfen*, which provides our sport in Germany with a face and a voice and has already been translated into English (as *Guide to Knife and Ax Throwing*). What could be read before that time either was from the Anglo-American realm (due to tradition) or wasn't up to the required level to provide real help and appropriate training manuals.

Luckily, the print media time and again show great interest. For newspapers, apparently the topic is exciting enough to at least report locally on various events and contests. I use any of these media-related chances to make our interesting and exciting sport more well known and to put it into perspective stepwise.

I also had this opportunity with the WDR, whose staff kindly produced a short portrait of me at the beginning of 2015 and thus gave me the opportunity to briefly introduce knife and ax throwing. A couple weeks later, I had a funny live interview with reporters of the WDR in front of the broadcasting center in Düsseldorf, Germany, for their program *Daheim und unterwegs* ("At home and on the road"). For me, these possibilities are very precious because they give me the chance to show the sportive throwing of weapons as exactly what it is in the end: a kind of sport. Nothing more, but nothing less either!

27 The Legal Side

Among the most-dangerous edged weapons existing are high-quality butcher and kitchen knives! Thus, if possible, avoid serious quarrels in the kitchen!"

(quote of a not entirely serious tip given by a police representative)

In the US, each state has ownership and carry laws that apply to knives. Generally speaking, most states permit the carry of pocket knives and multitools that have blades of less than 3 inches. Many US states also have restrictions on knives that have been deemed dangerous or as weapons (e.g., bowie knives). Overall, each state's and municipality's laws for the conceal and carry of knives will specify blade length and whether or not, for example, a switchblade has a lockable blade, which is usually illegal.

Throwing knives, which usually don't have sharpened edges, are generally not seen as knives, but as sports equipment. Thus they are not subject to weapons law. But you can't assume that every police officer is aware of this fine distinction.

For us sport throwers, this means in plain language that there is no comprehensible reason for having a throwing knife dangling from your hip and ready to be thrown while you are in a crowded pedestrian area or at a town fair. You should abstain from this to not provoke any trouble. As soon as you are on private grounds or in a training area, this legal carrying prohibition is irrelevant. For transporting knives to a training area or competition, they ought to be packed in a suitcase or similar suitable container. The possession of throwing knives at this time is neither criminal nor needs a special permit. Axes and tomahawks are not restricted at all, and neither are prohibited from carry.

In other countries the topic of knives is partly seen more stringently. The following is a brief overview of knife law in several European countries:

Austria: Austrians handle the topic of knives in an extremely liberal way. In practice there are no restrictions you would have to think about.

France: Meanwhile, the French thrower community is even larger than the German one, and there is a growing umbrella organization with many smaller societies. In France there are many world-class

Justitia—goddess of justice—always wears a blindfold as a symbol for being impartial (not looking at a person's reputation) and carries scales (for the judge) as well as an executioner's sword (verdict).
istockphoto.com/querbeet

Foto: istockphoto.com/querbeet

167

throwers, who have held official national championships once a year since 2008. In Germany this is still not the case. On the other hand, in France, carrying knives with fixed blades is prohibited completely and without exception. For carrying throwing knives there is the exemption rule of so-called "artistic" use. If this kind of permission is granted, then the corresponding throwing weapons are permitted to be owned and are allowed to be carried only in sportive training and competition.

Italy: The same is valid for our friends of the throwing sport in the land of pizzas and pasta. Carrying fixed blades is prohibited there by law, and it is recommended for us foreigners to always have the invitation for a throwing contest of a national organization with us. As an alternative, this is also valid for the membership card of the "Eurothrowers," which can be obtained for a yearly fee of ten euros. Until now this has always been accepted as a proof of artistic use of knives.

Great Britain: There are very strict laws for knives, which usually absolutely prohibit carrying any knives. Thus, always transport your throwing weapons in a lockable receptacle inside your suitcase or car trunk, so neither you nor anybody else has direct access to them. This rule also applies to France and Italy.

Switzerland: Here there is a need for a lot of missionary and elucidation work, because until recently, throwing knives were completely prohibited. Severe fines existed for violation of this Swiss weapons law. After the European championship of 2013 in the Czech village of Nivnice, a Swiss sport thrower was caught on his way back home; the man's knife was confiscated and he had to pay a fine of about 3,000 euros! He was even lucky, because the fine was actually required per weapon. But the officers found only one of his knives, not the other two. In that case he would have had to pay three times the amount.

Strangely, the possession of bayonets and axes has never been a legal problem in Switzerland, so Swiss throwers for a long time specialized in throwing bayonets. But in 2015, Swiss throwing friends and their supporters finally achieved a breakthrough: sportive knife throwing and the possession of throwing weapons are no longer illegal actions. Now our Swiss sport friends only have to manage to get throwing knives with symmetrical blades to become legal, because these are still prohibited.

Czech Republic: Totally liberal, and it's no problem to travel there.

When traveling to a French thrower contest in Roquefavour (Provence) in 2008, I got caught in a border check at the border between Germany and Luxembourg. The female officer on duty nicely asked why I wanted to travel to Luxembourg. This was a legitimate question because it was in the middle of the night.

I showed her a printout of the invitation of my French thrower friends to their contest. She asked, nicely again, whether I had my throwing knives with me. To this I replied—with my knowledge of French taught at school—that they were in the car trunk, and I would show them to her if required. She just smiled and indicated that this wasn't necessary. Instead she wished me success and luck in the competition. Result: with honesty and openness, you will always be able to score.

28 Gazing at the Crystal Ball

Within the years after the founding of the European umbrella organization "Eurothrowers," the number of friends of sportive knife and ax throwing, and thus the size of the thrower community in Europe, has grown enormously. Meanwhile, social media also provides a platform for exchanging experiences, selling material, facilitating dialogue between newbies and "old hands," and organizing small national thrower meetings and friendly competitions, as well as getting together. The German Facebook platform "Messer- und Tomahawkwerfen in Deutschland" ("knife- and tomahawk-throwing in Germany") currently has way above 400 members. This growth in interested people and new members has an influence on the international sportive scene and competitive landscape.

Time and again, fresh top talents appear out of nowhere and onto the stage of throwing-sport activity and deliver world-class performances. On the other hand, it is good to see that old "warhorses" from the foundation time are still around the front with their achievements.

In comparison: only fifteen active throwers participated in the first big European throwers meeting taking place at the western-style town of "Pullman City" in 2005. In 2014, the first world championship held on European grounds was in the French village of Callac, in a stadium filled to the brim with 4,500 spectators. At that time, more than 170 throwers competed for the title.

So a development can clearly be seen with respect to the steadily growing number of sportive throwers, but also with respect to the quality of performance. As is the case with all other kinds of sport, the sportive level of the thrower elite increasingly sets the bar higher. Results that would have been sufficient five years ago to confidently win in an international contest now almost make the participants tremble about whether they will be able to qualify for the finals.

From 2014 onward, with respect to the high number of participants, it became necessary to plan an additional day even to manage qualification contests. Since then, contests have started on a Friday morning and end with the awards ceremony late Sunday afternoon. In addition, the regulations in Europe were standardized in such a way that for each contestant in any European country, the same rules are valid, which was not the case in the middle of the previous decade.

I believe that our sport will probably never become an Olympic discipline, but maybe I am wrong. After all, the same was thought of the popular sports of snowboarding, mountain biking, beach volleyball, and skateboarding. I surely won't stick out my neck too far if I predict that the number of participants in a world cup in ten years will be at least 300 male and female throwers.

This means that from this point on, we will have to widen the time frame even more to be able to consider all participants. Or, as an alternative, we will have to introduce a qualification standard even to be able to participate in a big international event such as a European or world championship. Such standards already exist for other types of sport, and there they provide for a higher quality of sportive performance.

To introduce these standards, national competitions would be necessary where relevant performance has to be shown. The bearers of titles and the finalists of the previous year could always be qualified automatically to not overdo bureaucracy, because this is the same in other kinds of sport.

At the moment these mental games are still dreams of the future. Everything below 200 participants can still be managed without problems and within four days by means of streamlined organization, good weather, and a sufficiently large competition area.

Up to now, big and official international contests took place in the following countries: France, Italy, the US, Canada, Czech Republic, Great Britain, Hungary, and recently also a few times in Germany. So far, still more or less uninvolved are the Netherlands and Belgium (at this time, only one active contestant each). Both countries have very restrictive weapons laws, making things difficult for active throwers. It also looks meager for Spain, Austria, and the Scandinavian countries with the exception of Finland. In Hungary a growing thrower scene has started to become established.

For many years, Russia has had a comparatively large community with many active male and female throwers. Unfortunately, entry with our throwing weapons is subject to many governmental restrictions, which up to now have prevented the organization of big international contests in this country. But as you can see from the example of Switzerland, constant dripping wears away not only the stone, but sometimes even the tough, gray concrete of government offices.

The more well known our sport and its rules are and the more members and fans our sport scene wins, the easier it will be to loosen encrusted regulations and legal clauses in the long run and in our favor. For every sport thrower it pays off to actively participate in this.

29   A Few Closing Words

I hope that I managed to personally infect you with the virus of sportive knife throwing. I would be really happy if you were able to realize how much fun it can be to belong to our club of crazy steel throwers.

Here, at the end of this book, I wish to emphasize once more something to realize during practice and training: patience is the key! Patience, and in addition joy, a positive attitude, and a relaxed mind. After some time you will realize that throwing gives a lot in return. The investment for starting is not high with respect to finances or to training. The joy of moving outdoors in fresh air and of positive experiences in training will surely surprise you.

We sport throwers are approachable and uncomplicated buddies, so in case you have further questions (which may not have been answered by the contents of this book), don't hesitate to ask one of us or even me, be it via social networks, mail, or a phone call. We always like to help.

And if you feel fit enough for one of our contests, go ahead! Simply sign up, drive to the place of activity, and we will meet there! We all will welcome you among us and in our world of flying steel.

The Author

Peter Kramer (born 1964) is a passionate knife and ax thrower. Since 2005, the former springboard and high-board diver, as well as a wearer of the black belt in karate, has been performing this unusual sport within the European umbrella organization "Eurothrowers." Among other victories, he achieved six wins in the European championships of knife and ax throwers and numerous placements in the finals and

on the rostrum. The highlight of his career so far was the title of world champion with the throwing ax in 2015. He also achieved a world cup bronze placement with the throwing knife the same year. Peter Kramer is a frequent guest on German TV (*1, 2 oder 3, Kopfball, Countdown—die Jagd beginnt, Danni Lowinski, Galileo Fake Check*, and *Wilsberg*), where he performs on request as a knife and ax thrower and also counsels as an expert.

Tips by the World Champion

Peter Kramer achieved six wins in the European championships in knife and ax throwing and the title of world champion in ax throwing in 2015. In this book he provides precious tips for prospective knife and ax throwers with respect to getting into throwing and preparing for their first competitions. He introduces suitable throwing knives and axes and explains various throwing techniques as well as the legal conditions and proper maintenance of knives and axes. Last but not least, he also focuses on the mental aspects of knife and ax throwing during competitions.